I0797955

Praise for Bill Arnott's Books

"A gentle and fresh illustrative, sensory journey of festive memories for readers who enjoy cozy but not sugar-coated observations, unrushed thoughts, and portrayals of landscapes and characters on our unique and special west coast and Island."

—Anny Scoones, author of *Home and Away*, *True Home*, *Hometown*, *Last Dance in Shediac*, and *Island Home*

"If you're looking to be wrapped up in the warmth and wonder of the holiday season, Bill Arnott's *A Festive Season on Vancouver Island* is an absolute treat. The writing is beautifully engaging – it captures the magic of winter on the Island in such a vivid and heartfelt way."

—Nicola North, visual artist

"Anyone who even considers capturing Vancouver Island's holiday season in words needs not just a sharp eye but also a reflective mind. Bill Arnott has these in spades. He manages to make the reader feel fully immersed not just in the festivals of the season but also in an island steeped in history and thick with misty forests and wheeling gulls, the whole effect amplified by his distinctive illustrations. He gives depth and breadth to a richly diverse evocation of the darkest – and brightest – time of year."

—Theo Dombrowski, author of *Family Walks and Hikes of Vancouver Island*, *Popular Day Hikes Vancouver Island*, and *Seaside Walks on Vancouver Island*

A FESTIVE SEASON ON VANCOUVER ISLAND

A FESTIVE SEASON ON VANCOUVER ISLAND

BILL ARNOTT

RMB

First Edition

For information on purchasing bulk quantities of this book, or to obtain media excerpts or invite the author to speak at an event, please visit rmbooks.com and select the "Contact" tab.

RMB | Rocky Mountain Books Ltd.
rmbooks.com
@rm_books
facebook.com/rmbooks

Cataloguing data available from Library and Archives Canada
ISBN 9781771607261 (hardcover)
ISBN 9781771607278 (electronic)

Edited by: Kelly Laycock
Proofread by: Peter Enman
Design: Lara Minja, Lime Design

Printed and bound in China

We acknowledge the financial support of the Government of Canada through the Canada Book Fund and the Canada Council for the Arts, and of the province of British Columbia through the British Columbia Arts Council and the Book Publishing Tax Credit.

To the season, loved ones,
and every iteration of family.

Port McNeill
Tofino

VANCOUVER ISLAND

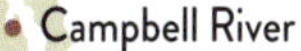

CONTENTS

ON AIR

INTRODUCTION

A Festive Playlist

I'm driving through light, under skyscraping cranes lit with festive red greens. All around are buildings in ice blue and white, their appearance both cozy and cool. Shiny ornaments sit by an office, awaiting a tree, as hedges and lampposts are dusted with garland and traffic-bulb tones. The vehicle pings, letting me know that it's freezing outside, while the sky is a sweater in black, twilight dark, as I drive to a big diesel boat. My destination: Vancouver Island.

The radio's tuned to Victoria, today commemorating the death of Shane MacGowan, singer for the Celtic punk band the Pogues. Then the ring of his tenor strikes my ears in a tumble of gravel as the station plays his song "Fairytale of New York" – what might be the most evocative festive song ever.

There's no one around and I stop the car to visit with Gayle, seated in a warm ticket booth, ahead of the ferry. She teases me about my getting a senior's rate soon. I admit I can't wait. Then ask her, "What's festive season mean to you?"

She looks through the dark, the space with no cars. Thinks a moment, then says, "The gathering of people I love."

I nod. Succinct, yet complete. We both smile, and I carry on. It's late November and the festive season has already begun. No more Halloween, tombstones in yards, or small candy bars. Thanksgiving sales are done, on both sides of the border. Now the prevalent aura is one of bright lights and song. MacGowan's "Fairytale" fades out. I spin the dial and two stations are already playing nothing but carols, some familiar, some new. Sure enough, without prompting, the season regurgitates background scores. José Feliciano wishing us "Feliz Navidad." Mariah Carey admitting that all she wants for Christmas is me. While Andy Williams insists "It's the Most Wonderful Time of the Year." He ought to know, he's been adamant about it for years.

As a child, a teen, a young adult, I spent most of December working at Dad's retail jewellery store. Festive season was the most important. Twelve-hour days, nine to nine, for a month, leading up to the 24th, when the store finally closed for two days. Most of the years I worked there we had two festive cassettes, which we'd rotate on a portable stereo. No streaming music, no cable. Just Andy Williams and Bing Crosby. And so my association with Andy belting out his declaration treads a delicate line between happiness and something adjacent to trauma.

But the season's distinct. In my opinion, most often lovely. Not necessarily linked to calendar months or a solstice, but more a notion or sentiment shared. Which brings us to this. You may know of these Season books. The first being *A Season on Vancouver Island*, in which my wife, Deb, and I went for a five-week vacation that lasted three months. Ninety days of unbroken sunshine, working remotely while exploring new places. Then I did it again. Spending *A Season in the Okanagan*, where I grew up, working those days in December. A place of good weather, orchards and vineyards, a deep string of lakes, with Indigenous history linking the pulse of each season.

Now, venturing out once again, the season is entirely new. Again, more a concept than a time frame. Some equate this season with religion or faith. For others it's the same as it was at our jewellery store, a time to "make hay" in the retail world. Here in the northern hemisphere, it's a time of cold weather. Near the coast, frequent rain. In the mountains, more snow. When skiers can do what they love.

I can't help but chuckle as I listen to another carol on the radio. Artists, perhaps, writing songs for residuals – a joke exploited in the movie *Love Actually*, the aging songwriter rebooting a classic, getting fresh airplay. Although I hadn't thought of this when Rocky Mountain Books asked if I'd revisit our Season series in this manner, to create a festive excursion. I thought it was a great idea. An opportunity to connect with old friends, make new ones as well, and to share it again in this manner. A privilege, to be sure. And a chance to feature more visual art, my painted photos from another new season, again in this magical place that embraced us that first time around. Vancouver Island. Connected, and yet set apart. Accessible, but requiring some effort, assuming you don't live here year-round. Maybe that heightens the allure. That, and the region's rare flora and fauna, layers of settler and Indigenous culture and history. All in diverse geography: mountains and forests, with endless expanses of shoreline.

Another smile. Maybe I *am* creating a kind of "Christmas Album," being on Vancouver Island for another new season. This one to celebrate the most festive time of the year, with or without Andy Williams. So I'm eager. An abundance of stories to revisit and share. Again, a rare pleasure. With the timing now perfect, because I have an appointment to keep, west of the Salish Sea, on the southeast of Vancouver Island. A play, where I have a seat near the stage, to one side. It's a radio play performed in a theatre, a fresh adaptation of *It's a Wonderful Life*. But with no

Jimmy Stewart or black and white film. Instead, a playhouse of actors on a stage in Chemainus.

The forecast is a mix of wet flurries, cold rain, and slush: slow going on roads, extra caution. With everything that I relish, an adventure, while still close to home. My alternate home. To experience a new season – a special one too. *A Festive Season on Vancouver Island.* ❖

LIGHT SHINING THROUGH DARK

The season begins in a monochrome. Gulls against overcast sky. From the ferry I drive onto the Island, Departure Bay shrinking behind me. The dark of pre-morning has faded, coloured lights on the buildings now softened, mostly turned off, waiting to come back to life in the late afternoon. I'm bisecting forested hills, driving south through Nanaimo, the sea a short distance away. Stopping for coffee, I visit with Angie, the barista who's making my latte, and return to our theme, asking what the festive season might mean to her.

"Oh, I don't know," she says, furrowing her brow. "Celebrating with family, more than anything, I suppose." She nods as she says it, solidifying her answer.

A ship's horn haunts the water. Finally, a hinting of colour, a thumbprint of peach on the horizon. Ice crystals dust hills in white smudges. There's a hank of thick fog. Bearing southeast, still in Nanaimo, a strong swirl of wind. The car gives a shimmy, a rock to the roll, as I navigate a curve in the highway. A spinning sensation. Reminding me of that summertime journey, the one that kept going, affirming the Island as another new home.

That time I watched a ferry pierce a dense wall of weather, a vertical line of misty sea-rain, as though a drape had been drawn halfway across the Salish Sea. Indigo grey to one side, on the other, a creamy expanse of azure. Watching the blue-and-white boat emerge from the gloom made me feel I was watching the technicolour transition of Dorothy escaping the Kansas tornado, leaving her old home behind to find solace and adventure in a wondrous, reimagined domain.

This time I stop by a beach, where I visit with the only other person around. The two of us a pair of lone wanderers, bound by shared landscape. Wind is still gusting, a squall off the water. It's cold in the bluster and wet. We share smiles, a quick chat. Discuss the season and weather while stamping our feet, blowing air on our hands. Then we part ways with a wave.

Now the beach feels abandoned, and I take it all in. A monstrous deadhead bobs near the shore, the look of a whale at rest. No wonder that leisurely drift of a whale is called "logging." Preparing, perhaps, for a deep ocean dive. Beyond, a squat tug hauls a barge, metal containers in white. Smoke wafts through dense trees up a mountain. A signal? A hermit preparing a meal? On the water there's a seamline of currents, as though the surface is mid quilting bee. A small jet passes over, banking hard, to descend to the south.

Now I'm backtracking to carve through more streets in Nanaimo. At the port, the Gabriola ferry is chunking its way through the water. A short distance south is the Helijet pad, flights suspended today because of high wind. I watch the small ferry ease into a dock, its wake a wide frothy vee, melding chop with the mist. The vista reminds me of a Pytheas quote, from his journey 25 centuries ago as he sailed the Arctic, referring to this type of watery scene as a "sea lung," living and breathing, each turn of wave an exhale. I can't help but see that same wake as a curtain, now open, recollections in charcoal and teal.

Another stop, another coffee, another visit with strangers, or rather, new friends. This time with Ethan and Dawn, the two travelling together, heading to Courtenay and Comox. Both hold ukuleles. Clearly a mentor-mentee relationship: Ethan, the young teacher, and Dawn, the student, perhaps twice his age. She strums and plucks strings. We chat music, and holidays. Eventually I ask what the festive season means to the two of them.

"Family," Dawn says almost instantly. A nod. Conclusive. Complete.

"Yeah," Ethan agrees, drawing out his reply, as though still formulating opinion. "I'd say pretty much the same thing. Getting together with people."

I glance at the sheet music Dawn's working on. Bobby McFerrin. "Don't Worry, Be Happy." And I smile, as this takes me back to the road when I drove next to Lake Okanagan, another bridging of seasons. I finish my coffee and bid them both well. Fellow travellers sharing a musical score.

Our encounter reminds me of another trek here, to Nanaimo, with my own music mentor, named Michael. The same sensei and friend I reconnected with for that Okanagan season – two seasons, in fact, our time together straddling summer and fall. But it was this time of year, dark and damp, when we came to Nanaimo for a gig. Each of us toting guitars: six-string acoustics, steel strings. The coil of the strings felt like ice, demanding to play in the cold. But we persevered. Shared a stage with storytellers and poets in a dim bar by the harbour. High-topped tables with candles emitted a feeling of time warps and beatniks.

After, we walked to a friend's through mizzle and murk, to spend the night in their home. I'd say we sofa-surfed, but in truth I was surfing their floor. Michael, who's tall, was jammed into a child's bed, performing a cirque-like contortion. It felt like a middle school sleepover, and we went to sleep laughing.

Today, Nanaimo harbour is jammed with container ships. I want to believe they're all stuffed with toys, sea-sleighs of Santa with stevedore elves. The sun's trying to shine, struggling through layers of grey. A long hooting ship's horn rolls on the water. *FWWOOOOO!* A rumble of cars rattles past. No doubt a ferry disgorging, a leviathan spitting out krill.

Back in the car, I drive south, down the east side of the Island, past a sign that reads: *Nanaimo. The Harbour City.* The new season is starting with frost, chill sea air, and low mist, the temperature just above freezing. A few beams of light strike the trees and the inlet. I pass Newcastle Marina and Boatyard, into the south of Nanaimo. Waterfront hotels and suites. A gull wheels over, outlined in sun, a photographer's dream. I fight the urge to reach for my camera, tending instead to the slick of the road.

I circle back, finding different perspectives. The Sand Dollar Manor. Sands Funeral Chapel. A ferry to Newcastle Island. I could simply read signs to confirm that I'm waterside. But with a window ajar I can sense it as well. Aroma of tide, cry of seabirds.

Past another marina, where docks merge in ells, moored boats tethered near seaplanes. On a branch of the highway, late season road repairs are slowing traffic, now funnelling into one lane. *Expect delays.* The wave of a worker, stop sign and flag.

The leisurely pace lets me soak up my surroundings. I spot a back-alley entryway, next to a dumpster. Its signage reads *Private Wealth Management*. A boarded-up building is tagged with a scrawl of fresh paint: *Housing is healthcare*. A message that resonates. A few unhoused residents on corners, crossing the street. I veer toward the water, bump across a low bridge, then railway tracks. Past a boatyard and dry dock. Onward through residential neighbourhoods with tree-lined streets and green yards. Deflated decorations flop on a roof, a pancaked Santa and flat Christmas tree, the jolly duo in need of a sea lung or two.

I steer clear of the main thoroughfare to experience more of the town in the season. Learning of local light-up fanatic Rohn Brown, I drive by the house where he lived with his partner Dianne. Off Rutherford Road, I follow the side street of Sams Way, where the Brown house illuminated the area for years, literally, their front yard a blaze of bright twinkle. Brown was known as the "neighbourhood mayor," and his home served as a beacon. His festive passion was what one might expect from Clark Griswold in *National Lampoon's Christmas Vacation*, the film making the joy of "exterior illumination" an expression synonymous with the season. When Rohn passed away, his family paid tribute by decorating the house and the yard once again in the manner he treasured. Much like love, light shining through dark. ❖

AROMA OF RESIN AND PINE

As I drive through residential neighbourhoods – lighting on homes strung with garland – I'm reminded of childhood again, this time of year. A fresh-cut evergreen in the house, aroma of resin and pine. Rummaging through storage for ornaments and boxes of lights. For me, growing up, this was predominantly a secular occasion. Retail shopping, gift wrapping, books and new toys, with festive music blaring from every sound system. School holidays. Hopefully snow. Skiing and cocoa, mittens and toques. Additional food, and rest.

As I researched what this time of year means to most people in this part of the world, what surfaced immediately were non-religious traditions: family gatherings, decorations, giving gifts, singing carols, reading books, baking, along with volunteering and charitable donations. All of which I felt I was already experiencing, or hearing about, to a degree. I also learned a sliver of history around the decorative tree in a house. It was originally a pagan ritual, a fir tree representing ongoing life and fertility.

Candles would light up the boughs, reminders of brightening days ahead, an eventual end to the darkness of northern hemisphere winters.

For those celebrating from a Christian perspective, most acknowledge the birth of Jesus shifting on the calendar to coincide with long-running traditions of yuletide. With seasonal activities attributed to Germanic peoples, expanding to Scandinavia and across western Europe, yule is associated with the Wild Hunt, a blend of folklore, myth, and practicality. When late autumn hunting was at its peak, game animals would be moving in herds, fattened for winter, prime for harvesting and preparing for storage in cold temperatures. The folklore relates to the myth that the hunt was originally led by the gods, usually Odin (from Norse mythology), also called Woden (in Old English). Consistent with the belief that higher powers provide, and our day-to-day lives should acknowledge our blessings. A time of abundance, and gratitude.

The next bit of research I find pertains to atheists, non-believers in a god or in gods. Some celebrate *Newtonmas* on December 25th, named for Sir Isaac Newton, as that was his birthday. A tidy calendar tie-in combined with acknowledging "science" in lieu of religion or faith, irrespective of bright lights and "Christmas" trees.

Many churchgoers will decorate with a crèche or nativity scene. Imagery or models representing the birth of Jesus, usually with gift-giving wisemen or magi, livestock depicting a stable, with the biblical figures of Mary and Joseph. Gabriel is often in attendance as well, the angel credited with informing Mary that she was expecting and that the world would forever be changed.

I even learned a bit more about Santa Claus, an adaptation of the legendary gift-giving statesman from northern and western Europe, Sinterklaas. Who in turn was based on Saint Nicholas, a Greek Christian bishop from Turkey, credited with numerous miracles, thereby earning the moniker of "wonderworker." Nicholas is the patron saint of a great many things: sailors, archers, merchants, brewers, pawnbrokers, thieves who no longer steal, single people, and exchange students as well. But most notably, Saint Nick is patron saint of children, known for his great snowy beard, a red hat, and a penchant for giving gifts to well-behaved kids. If those children lived in a house with a chimney, that was often how the wonderworker gained access.

Now, by skirting compass points as I drive, I'm able to engage with a broader swath of community. A bit south, a bit west, I stop at the Islamic Centre of Nanaimo, a hub for mid-Island Muslims. Birds are chirping in pines, and the front door is framed by a fig tree and Jerusalem artichoke. I buzz the imam, hoping to gain insight on the season from the perspective of followers of Muhammad. I'm aware of the prophet's birthday, celebrated near fall equinox. And Ashura, when Moses, it's said, divided the Red Sea. As well as the fasting of Ramadan, then the feasting of Eid, taking place in the spring. But that's all anecdotal, things I've read or heard second-hand.

The first intimate experience I had with Islam arose when I made new friends in college, my best Muslim mate being Khaled, from Libya. We'd watch the news every night, as his hometown was bombed, repeatedly, by the Bush administration du jour. Then he'd call the next day, if the phone lines were working, to see if his family was alive.

Mom insisted Khaled join us for Christmas, proudly cooking a feast. The feature was glazed ham, which I'm certain, despite my ignorance, wasn't halal. Khaled, however, remained an ambassador for decorum, thanking us for such generosity, then filling up on steamed veg and mash. With a discreet tumbler of wine.

At the mosque, those in attendance are presently busy with prayer, a mixture of motion and silence, and I tiptoe back through the greenery, out to the car, admiring their dedication and faith. But I follow up with Randa, who runs a local Islamic school.

To my pleasant surprise I was invited to take part in the students' poetry festival, celebrating the work of Rumi, the prolific Muslim poet and scholar from the 13th century. Ahead of the event I'm reminded, warmly but firmly, that singing is not part of the reading. *Prayers* are sung. Poetry, however, is savoured through reading, the inherent cadence of metre and rhyme its own invocation.

From the mosque, I drive a short distance to the local *chabad*, which serves as community synagogue, a home on a hill with a view of the water. Here I visit with Blumie, community leader and spouse of the local rabbi. I've arrived during Torah lessons, the comings and going of parents and kids. In the yard is a shiny menorah, aluminum glinting in wan light through the cloud. Faux lights top the branches of the menorah, and a wasp trap hangs from one side. Could it be that's a joke? Intended to attract a few WASPs? I make a mental note to ask Rabbi Bentzi when I see him, and to get his insight on what's funny and what's simply offensive. But the feeling is certainly festive. Hanukkah is about to commence, a time of presents and lights, seasonal feasting and a gathering of loved ones.

I chat with Jennifer, who's heading in for a lesson, and learn of the meaning of *chabad* with respect to Judaism. In fact, it's an acronym for the three religious and philosophical traits of *chochmah*, *binah*, and *daat*. Wisdom, understanding, and knowledge. Where we are, next to the menorah in the centre of the lawn, the yard is bookended in rhododendron and pine, with an enormous blue spruce to one side, like a magus awaiting companions.

A short drive away, two turns past a park, I arrive at the city's gurdwara, the Sikh temple, lined in a thick hedge of blackberry. A few well-aged firs give the high land the look of a cake, the pines like regal green candles. I was hoping to ask the Granthi, reader of scriptures and leader of prayer, about the season as well, but the building is now cordoned off, under repair. Caution tape wraps the front stairwell, leading up to two rounded facades. The ribbons of yellow almost add a festive appearance, garland in low-carat gold.

Another memory plays out, once more from college, although a different school, different time. When I joined a campus club and became friends with Harjit, or Harj, and learned a bit more of Sikhism. It was autumn when we met, and Diwali was happening, the festival of lights, a celebration recognized by numerous faiths. In the dharma of Hinduism, for example, the observance is associated with Lakshmi, goddess of prosperity, the reigning of light over darkness, or knowledge conquering ignorance.

For Harj and his family, worshipping at the local Sikh temple, the festival represented a historical struggle for freedom. To celebrate Guru Hargobind's victory over imprisonment from Emperor Jahangir, which occurred in the 17th century. Diwali at the gurdwara, therefore, was recognized by the lighting of the Golden Temple, which happens in Amritsar, India, again a festival of light, symbolized regionally by igniting decorative oil lamps called *diyas*. Although it's most frequently observed in October and November, my friend told me many people he knew would extend commemorations into December, therefore coinciding with a wealth of comparable festivals.

Seeking knowledge, reflection, and wisdom. Lighting candles and lamps. Enjoying festive meals. Gathering and sharing with loved ones, living and passed. Many versions of much the same thing.

DREAMING OF SNOW

Another wide loop through town, where a man walks a malamute, the dog pulling its owner while dreaming of snow. From a loft in the highway, I glimpse the near-perfect oval of Newcastle Island. Past the visitor centre, where posters for tours flap in a breeze. Foggy hills to the west, arbutus interspersed with tall pines. The local radio station announces Light the Trees is happening now, supporting the Nanaimo & District Hospital Foundation, and that a helpline is active, part of the mental health crisis resources they offer. Next to the road, a bouquet of fresh flowers, an unmarked memorial.

Back into residential, one- and two-storey homes. Another yard with deflated ornaments, pancakes of snowmen and elves. Hockey nets frame a cul-de-sac, a street rink in concrete. Rain speckles the windshield, barely enough for the wipers, more of a sea mist than rain. The radio broadcasts a public service announcement: road safety reminders. And the on-air personality poses a question, "What are you doing to make the festive season less stressful?"

I expect it to ease into ads for prepared meals or shopping, but no, just filling airtime between songs.

Then a string of sopranos serenades me from town: Kelly Clarkson, Selena Gomez, Taylor Swift. As I mull the notion of a festive season, considering the places of worship I've come from, aptly enough Alanis Morissette joins the rotation, reminding me even *she* hasn't got it all figured out just yet. And so I keep going, a slightly open window and a predominantly open mind.

My route south takes me through a series of *C*s: Colvilletown, Cedar, Cassidy, and Chemainus, where I learn more layers of history. Colvilletown was a Hudson's Bay trading post, an overland service centre for furriers and couriers, until the mid-1850s, when coal took over, assuming lead role for commerce. In the Salishan language group known as Halkomelem, Snuneymuxw was the Indigenous name for the region, which settlers phonetically translated to Nanaimo, now encompassing this mid-eastern portion of the Island.

Between here and the water is Cedar, also known as Cedar by the Sea, another Coast Salish region infused with European arrivals when immigration expanded through the 19th century. A proliferation of western red cedar, in addition to rich seams of coal, drew loggers and miners and were the primary resources driving growth amongst settlers.

Now on both sides of the highway deciduous leaves are in gold, a sparkle of ore between evergreens. A sign reminds me I'm heading toward Ladysmith, past a pond, glassy calm, with black and brown cattle beyond. A raven flaps by next to WildPlay Element Park, where there's signage for ziplines and bungee.

More stands of hardwood and pine, bare branches amid needles of green. Past Nanaimo River Hatchery, where the road parallels a rail trestle. In the distance, an inn and a campground. Another rail crossing, the old Esquimalt & Nanaimo Railway, or E&N line. Now a turnoff to Nanaimo Airport, on Spitfire Way. And a tie-in to the history of Cassidy, named for Thomas Cassidy, known as the first settler farmer of seafood. It was here Cassidy started an oyster farm, growing it into an industry.

In the mid-1880s the railway was being completed to shuttle in workers, families, and equipment, and to haul out lumber and coal. Cassidy serviced the area, offering supplies, growing and selling fresh produce, and developing shellfish harvesting. It was this sprawl of acreage, reaching east to the sea, that was eventually sold by the family to the Department of National Defence, to be used by the Royal Canadian Air Force, the airstrip and land that's now Nanaimo Airport. The road forks and I continue south on Highway 1, the Trans-Canada. Past the

Western Maritime Institute and a lone boondocker parked in a field, an RV as big as a house. I pass logging trucks loaded with logs, each hunk of timber the size of a phone pole.

With memories of Cassidy's bivalves, I exit the highway to Oyster Bay Village, and call the place I'll be staying, a roadside motel. It's still early, but they tell me they're not busy and I'm welcome to check in anytime. It's the norm, they explain, at this time of year, the only guests being travelling athletes – swim teams and hockey. I steer between trees dressed in lights. Next to my lodging are a cannabis shop and a liquor store, and I consider extending my stay.

Strands of white lights are wrapping the motel's porte cochère. Rain adds a twinkle effect to the bulbs, making things even more festive. A few blue lights add a North Pole or toy-workshop feel. In the lobby, festive elves sit on shelves, dangling their soft fabric legs by a faux snow-dusted tree. A small girl is wheeling a trolley through the lobby. On the trolley are two smaller girls. The scene could be Whoville, and I can't help but imagine the two smaller girls each with their own even tinier trolleys and girls, and so on.

I have time to unpack, stretch my legs, before continuing south in the car, from Oyster Bay to Chemainus, once again crossing the E&N line. I skirt the town of Ladysmith, for now, but I'll return after dark for the Light Up Parade, a community kickoff to the season. By Bob Stuart Park a sign announces the parade with its accompanying event, Ladysmith's Festival of Lights.

A cenotaph stands in the cold, the stone looking chill in the weather, as though due for a scarf and a hat. Another truck and trailer loaded with lumber, this one stacked into two-by-four cubes. I pass stables and farms, everything seemingly huge. Fields in sere browns and greens, some fallow with low winter wheat, some tilled into corduroy lines. A sign reads *Entering North Cowichan* as rain picks up, the sky a dull grey. I head east toward Chemainus, exiting the highway, passing a Calvary Baptist Church en route to my pre-matinee lunch. There's a house with a picturesque veranda dressed in wreaths and red ribbons. It could serve as a prop for the play I'll see soon, a cheery version of George Bailey's hometown.

Here in Chemainus, I'm on Coast Salish land of the Stz'uminus First Nation, traditional territory that hugs the east side of the Island, edging north toward the Comox Valley. Like the towns I've just been to, this was a place of immigrant settlers drawn for industry and massive old trees. Lumber mills followed loggers. Towns followed mills. And soon the area boomed with new residents from Europe, China, and Japan. This swath of the Island was known as Chemainus Valley, with its hub, where

I am, housing multiple ethnicity centres. Two "Chinatowns." Two "Japantowns." People staffing the mills, constructing the railway. Retail supporting the workers. Until the especially dark period of government policy around the Second World War, both during and after, when Japanese-Canadian citizens were interned, or more accurately, incarcerated, province-wide.

In the heart of Chemainus I park and walk around, where a whiff of logging still clings, an aroma of pulp in the air. The valley's draped in a shawl of wet weather, icy and damp with a thick mist of rain. I stroll streets and the shore by a small ferry terminus. A squat ticket booth, a short lane for traffic, sailings to Thetis and Penelakut Islands.

At Jollity Farm Café a sign reads *Coffee + Tea + Used Books*, a warm invitation. Inside, I visit with Yuka, who's lived in Chemainus a few years, having moved, as she puts it, from "rural Tokyo." I admit I didn't realize there *was* a rural Tokyo. Yuka laughs.

"Have you been to Japan?" she asks.

I tell her I have, to Tokyo's heart and the thrum of Shibuya, before heading west to Kyoto.

"Ah, yes," she says with a nod. "So you *did* get a taste of the city and countryside too, some new and some old. Where I come from, outside of Tokyo, it's very beautiful. There's a hot spring."

"And how do you like it *here*?"

"Oh, it's very nice. Chemainus, the Island. Kind people." She pushes free food toward me. "Here, try this. It's dip, and crackers, all from our farm, out on Thetis. We use whatever is fresh."

The crackers are coarse grain, the colour of clementines, with a vibrant green dip made from basil. Today's soup is a borscht from red beets, completing the festive palette. Everything's sumptuous, my soup served with a slab of focaccia. I sit by a high wall of books, slurp my soup, and couldn't be happier.

At the next table a young girl reads a book to her parents, the energy in the space inspiring.

I visit with Suzanne, a traveller in transit, waiting for the ferry across the street.

"Oh, gotta go!" she says, glancing at her watch. "Thank you, Liz!" she shouts to the back of the store, where an owner is assembling produce.

"Thank you, Suzanne!" echoes from a walk-in cooler.

"I love your dress," another woman says.

"Oh my god," she replies.

"Yeah, oh my god!"

"I mean, Oh My God. The boutique on Salt Spring. That's where I got it."

"Oh my god!"

"Yeah, Oh My God."

Everyone waves, carries on.

From the café I walk through the village, across Croft Street to Old Town Chemainus, where people are gathering for the radio-play stage performance. The premise? Actors playing actors, playing a play. Performed as though live on the radio.

Ahead of the matinee, the cast comes on stage, in full costume, and visits with the audience. Introductions, interaction, a few questions, some banter and laughs. Not sure if it's always like this or because today's performance is "relaxed." A relaxed performance is much like it sounds. Less formal. A time in which *all* attendees are welcome. There's no shushing. Guests are welcome to come and go if they wish. Noise from the play is muted, houselights kept halfway on. There's less sensory vibrance on stage, the whole play being softened. The ideal performance for those requiring reduced stimulation, those sensitive to bright light and loud noise. Now the production company works to ensure at least one relaxed showing per run.

The play is good fun. The script the same as the Frank Capra film. But the radio-play angle offers slots for new jokes, with staged ads between scenes. What you'd expect from a live 1940s radio play. Funny products with catchy jingles, another chance for live music. Sound effects too. The "audio tech" doing things to create an aural experience: opening and closing a door. A bell. Stamping shoes on a board for footsteps. The *aaawwooogah* of a vintage car horn. I could actually close my eyes and experience it all like a radio show.

There's a touch of the British holiday pantomime, as audience members offer up an occasional shout of approval or dismay. Maybe because today's show is relaxed. The greatest interaction is to references of social relevance: affordable housing, immigration, mental health. Apart from some cringeworthy sexist and racist material, the story's as current as ever.

During intermission I sip cocoa and get to know Lena, a volunteer at the theatre. Now a Chemainus resident, Lena moved here from Salt Spring Island.

"Tell me how you like it here, this time of year."

"Oh, I love it," she says. "I lived in Manitoba before moving to Salt Spring. Been in Chemainus five years and just love it. Got tired of ferries. And it's friendly and positive here. I have no time for negative people." She looks out a window. "Winter gets dark pretty early, but the theatre is busy." She smiles. "And there's plenty of lights."

I return to my seat, a second hour slides by, and we finish with a singalong of "Auld Lang Syne." The crowd files out, and I wander through town a bit more, follow a path of yellow footprints, admire some murals, paintings of regional history. The weather is cool but pleasant, rain no more than a drizzle. I could carry on, strolling and admiring the art, maybe find another bowl of soup. But a parade is about to begin just down the road, and I plan to be there when it starts.

Centennial Square at Sunset, Victoria

Arbutus at Seabird Park, Victoria

Esquimalt Gorge Park

Esquimalt Lagoon, Colwood

University of Victoria Winter Choir in Christ Church Cathedral

The *Knowledge Totem*, carved by Cicero August and his sons Darrell and Doug August, near BC's Parliament Buildings

Outside the First Peoples Gallery at Royal BC Museum

HAPPY LIGHT-UP!

Bright-lit trees guide me out of Chemainus, slender updos in glimmering white. I can't tell the trees, something branchy and slim, the look of living lampposts. I pass a float on the highway, making its way to the parade route in Ladysmith, a flatbed adorned in white trees of bent steel. A small tractor, dressed as a reindeer, rumbles ahead at 90 kilometres per hour.

Getting to Ladysmith, I'm living the Chris Rea song "Driving Home for Christmas," his lyrical reference to tailbacks, meaning vehicle taillights, the same light-up I'm crawling through now. A long line of brake lights, festively red. An occasional pulse as we slowly advance. Everyone, it seems, on their way to Ladysmith's Light Up Parade.

Streets are blocked off, traffic diverted outside of downtown. I drive two kilometres south, park by a school, walk back with families and strollers, kids bundled up. A few umbrellas in spattering rain. The town's moniker, *A View to Sea*, couldn't be more fitting, as the centre slopes to the highway and shoreline.

I walk the same route the parade floats will follow and get to admire each glowing vehicle before they start moving. I snap a few photos. There's a Polar Express, now dark, a visual that could be straight from the book or the movie. I circle the train, admire the work.

"Want me to turn on the lights for you?" a man asks.

"That would be awesome!" I say, like a kid tearing open a present.

The man's name is Doug. He cranks a generator and the Polar Express fires to life, an explosion of silver and turquoise. I can imagine the delight in my eyes, a reflection of illumination and train. Total number of passengers: one. One very happy old traveller. I take photos, thank Doug, then he turns off the Polar Express, where it sits in the dark, waiting to start its next run.

I weave between people, the sidewalk, the street. Town centre is packed, awaiting the parade and the light-up. A saxophone is warming up in a school band, the brass honk of "Rudolph the Red-Nosed Reindeer." A sailboat is strung with high lights on a flatbed, as though the truck is the sea, a "boat afloat a boat-float."

As I reach the centre of town a loudspeaker booms, keeping kids entertained and distracted, awaiting the parade and the light-up. A singalong chorus, the same reindeer song as the saxophone. Now trivia.

"Do you know what the first Christmas tree lights were?" the voice from the speaker calls out.

Shouts from children, excitement and enthusiasm.

"It was actually candles, imitating the twinkling of stars!"

Some *oohs* and *ahhs*. A good crowd.

From passersby, the salutation is, "Happy Light-Up!" It becomes the go-to exchange.

"Happy Light-Up!"

"Happy Light-Up."

Over a curry, I visit with Lauren, who works here, and ask what the season means to her.

"Oh, all of this," she says, indicating the people, the lights. "Celebration. The city parade." She thinks about it some more, then adds, "And family. Getting together with people you love."

Martin, the owner, comes out from the kitchen where he's been working the stovetop and grill, chats everyone up, in spite of the crush, making sure we're all happy. It's a breakfast and lunch-time place, but Martin's staying open to show his support, like every retailer in town. A proper community event. Families march through, loading up on hot chocolate. A few hurried diners like me. Outside, people are munching from takeaway cartons, lining the street four- and five-deep for the entire parade route.

Outside, I talk to Jim, one of the parade organizers and a Kin club volunteer, and ask him about the event.

"Been doing it 14 years, for as long as I've been with Kin. And lived here all my life."

"What's the highlight for you?" I ask.

"Oh, *all this*. Doing it for the community. Giving back. The beers afterward taste awfully good too," he says with a smile. "Gotta deal with one broken-down float, though, before we get going. Would you believe it? The BC Ferries float." He laughs, a great rattling guffaw. "Who would've thought?!" He rolls his eyes, laughs again, then shakes my hand and heads off to jumpstart a ferry on wheels.

The energy's growing, the parade starting soon. The Polar Express is now filled with kids. A church float has upbeat hymns cranked. A float with a crèche sits next to a jail being hauled by the BC Sheriff Service. Inside the jail, peering through bars, are a dozen tiny convicts, children in striped jumpsuits. Clearly the naughty ones. Apparently, times have changed since coal lumps in stockings.

I keep strolling, facing the line of parked floats, lights agleam, awaiting the "go" sign from Santa – my own solo parade in reverse.

A pack of children has just stormed the Coca-Cola truck, a blue-lighted tractor and trailer.

"I unlocked it!" a little voice shouts.

"Yay!!!" A chorus of squeals as a clamber of small bodies floods the cab of the semi, a swarm of cherubic looters in wool toques and red-sparkled antlers. I keep walking, not wanting to be around when they figure out how to fire up the engine.

Turning a corner, I come to a house and yard engulfed in light, outlines of snow people, stars in purple and amber. The place resembles the Brown home in Nanaimo, another tribute to fans of exterior illumination.

The blast of an airhorn echoes behind me, and I wonder if it's the signal to start the parade or if the renegade gang from the Coke truck figured out how to hotwire their ride.

The drizzle of rain abates, the downtown lights up, and the parade is another success. Fireworks cap off the evening, and I take my leave ahead of the unending vehicle lines, one heading north and one south.

By my accommodation, I visit with Stewart, a man of very few words.

"Tell me what the festive season is to you," I say, as though coaxing a mime to speak up.

"Hmm. Spending time with quality friends, and family."

Which I like. Not quality *time* per se, but quality *friends*.

Back in my room, the original *Grinch* is on TV, and I sing along to the opening, with all the Whos down in Whoville, the tall and the small. And remarkably, right on cue, as the Grinch on TV complains of the "Noise, noise, noise, noise!" a pack of children go thundering down the hall. I wonder if they're swimmers or a hockey team. Then I discover something wondrous. As the Grinch is getting on with his home invasions, slithering through living rooms, stealing groceries and toys, I put the TV on mute, and instead play "Fairytale of New York," which scores the scene perfectly.

THE FEEL OF A BROTHERS GRIMM TALE

I've gotten in touch with Carol, one of the organizers of Duncan's festive Christmas Express train at the BC Forest Discovery Centre, as I plan to continue around the Island, attending events as I go. I figure I can get in on one of the train's first runs of the season, earlier in the day, mid-afternoon, to get ahead of the crowds.

"Oh," Carol says. "Oh, dear. No, I'm afraid we're completely sold out. Have been for weeks."

Wonderful news for the sponsors, attendees and hosts, but a bit disappointing for me. I'd checked previously and figured I had a shot at a ticket, but no. Lesson learned, with kudos to the team here in Duncan. In the meantime, I'll savour memories of Doug running the Polar Express for my private excursion.

In lieu of a festive train ride, I circle back for the opening of Nanaimo's Christmas Village, being held at the German Cultural Centre. Once more I'm in the pleasantly tight undulation of land that houses the Sikh and Islamic temples, along with the *chabad* and two churches. The morning has turned into drizzle with mist in high and low bands, and I see a long line of cars, the same look as the taillights that led me through Ladysmith.

I park a ways from the venue on a precipitous incline, crank the handbrake, and traverse a narrow road like a black-diamond ski slope. A small bridge crosses Millstone River, where a froth of whitewater bends in an elbow under a canopy of wonderfully red and green trees. Between the gorge and the forest and gloom of the day, it feels like a Grimm Brothers tale. Maybe that's the appeal of this locale, river and hills like the edge of Bavaria, one of the first homes of Sinterklaas.

Out front of the compact Cultural Centre a marquee is set up, vendors and welcoming hosts. Inside, the space is indeed a tribute to Germany. Deutschland paintings of landscapes and historical buildings next to a Berlin Bear. I buy a sausage-in-a-bun, extend a *guten tag*, and fight the urge to burst into "Edelweiss."

The space is jammed with an array of artisan crafts, knit goods and woodwork, with heaps of baked stollen. I shuffle about with the crowd, then visit with Bridget.

"How do you like this time of year?"

"Oh, it's busy, but I like it," she says. Bridget's in charge of the baking, a huge task for an intense period of time.

Next I chat with a woman named Sylvia, standing next to a table of handcrafted wood: burls polished in whorls, with custom guitar picks, fine-grained bookmarks, and placemats. Reminders of my slim disc of alder, another touchstone from seasons elsewhere.

Half the conversations are in German, everyone in a warm festive mood. I browse a few paintings and visit with the artist, her pieces hand-blown floral designs. The display an array of wildflowers and poinsettias in a palette of yellow and blue, reminiscent of sunflowers and irises.

The crowd thickens, and I extricate myself from the throng. Back over the river, up the slope to the car, where ads on the radio announce the light-up of Qualicum's Milner Gardens and Woodland, a weekend affair with a teahouse.

On the main road, traffic slows for a funeral procession, a long row of cars, hazard lights flashing, a dark hearse at the head of the line. Heavy cloud sits directly on mountains, each topped with a froth of dark fog. Another radio ad, Lights of Wonder has officially begun at Victoria's Centennial Square, which I'll see for myself soon enough.

Jupiter rises in the darkening sky. There's another glimmer of light through the mist on the water. A vessel? A lighthouse? I never do learn what it is, and part of me likes that it lingers in mystery. Turning the vehicle south, I'm off to connect with Deb at Swartz

Bay, the ferry terminal near Sidney. From there we'll explore the bottom end of the Island together while I do my best to keep up with the season. ❁

CULTURE IN CARVINGS OF WOOD

A new morning, today with bright sun, and I'm aware of more decorations. More houses with lights, hanging snowflakes, inflated figurines standing in yards. Deb and I are in the vehicle, touring the south of the Island. At the moment we're driving past Saanich Historical Artifacts Society, where an old train is curled on the grass like a slug in hot sun. Concrete pillars poke from the road, an overpass under construction. Walkers on footpaths carve their way through the woods by Elk Lake. Beaver Lake too. While a lone cyclist shares the trail, bundled against the chill.

Eventually some signage, a seagull and anchor. *Welcome to Greater Victoria*. Thin dark cloud accompanies sunshine, weaving and waving in ribbons, bringing the sunlight to life. Lamas and sheep graze in farms as a raven flaps over. A red-apple tree leans by the road, branches of festive fruit baubles. A gibbous moon peers through some cloud, and a flocking of birds I don't know swirls into spirograph shapes.

We skirt downtown Victoria to start the day in Vic West and Esquimalt. A stop at Midwood Beach and then Seabird Park at the head of Victoria's Gorge Tillicum neighbourhood, where a snowberry hedge circles the space, white berries dangling like miniature snowpeople.

Aptly enough, seagulls rest on a log on the Seabird Park inlet, and we watch a low amber sun warm the arbutus trees' coppery tones. Back in the car we cross bridges spanning the Gorge. This is Esquimalt and Songhees land, the First Peoples having used this finger of sea for harvesting herring, salmon, and oysters, as well as ducks, geese, and the remarkably versatile eelgrass. The grain of this shallow saltwater plant can be used like wild rice. Its tender green shoots are a fragrant addition for curing and smoking meats. When dried, it's a fine insulation for stuffing or making a mattress. Where it grows it attracts fish and ducks, a super-flora like cedar. You can feed and clothe a family with it, and it never stops giving.

Following the establishment of Fort Victoria in 1843, a passenger ferry ran here, bringing settler residents up through the Gorge as an accessible swim destination. A diving platform was built, the waterway considered, in a way, its own "relaxed" environment. Settler class distinctions were, more or less, left elsewhere. People bathed here and swam, soaked up sun and socialized. Regattas and picnics were common and frequent, with the ferry acting as a shuttle, people flagging it down as it made its way back and forth from here to the mouth of the harbour.

Sightseers also took this route to visit the "reversing falls" at the Gorge Narrows, by what's now Tillicum Road Bridge, overlooking the Victoria Canoe and Kayak Club. Under the burble of water are what's left of two prominent rocks. According to Indigenous legend, the stone stubs are the remains of a young girl named Camossung and her grandfather.

The story goes that the Transformer, a spirit-being known to many Pacific Coast Nations, encountered the girl by the water. She was upset, and hungry. Apparently, she was a picky eater and her grandfather had grown impatient. The Transformer, known as Haylas in this area, offered Camossung an array of food, which the girl refused to eat. The only things she enjoyed were duck and salmon, herring and oysters. And so, to ensure these foods would remain and be sustainably managed, Haylas turned Camossung and her grandfather into the stones where the water is frothiest. A reminder too, perhaps, to appreciate the food that's on offer.

Farther west, just off the Old Island Highway, we make a leisurely loop around Esquimalt Lagoon.

Waves thrash the beach, driftwood and timber tossed high on the shore. The Fisgard Lighthouse at Fort Rodd Hill looks on, red and white, from its promontory. A couple is walking three dogs, everyone in their party adorned in raingear. Gulls hang in the wind. In the lagoon, ducks paddle and dive.

From here we circle Fort Rodd Hill, where pumpkins sit by the road like a line of orangey round hitchhikers. Heading west, through hills of grey-black Garry oak, along an open expanse of the Salish Sea, clouds thicken, forcing sun to persevere through the overhead muck. We pass Witty's Lagoon and Tower Point, then make our way to Bilston Creek Farm, where a holiday market is now underway.

We park at the farm, the grounds today in celebratory flair. Stroll under apple trees, branches still loaded with fruit, the festive look of holly with berries. A monstrous arbutus centres the property, with lavender fields in perfect round shrubs. The bushes could pass for a gelato shop, scoop after scoop, every option in one floral flavour.

Inside the market, a beautifully recrafted barn, I strike up conversation with Crystal, part of a team of four generations of bakers, and ask about the season.

"I love it!" she says, eyes agleam. "It's baking time!"

I buy my second breakfast, a sausage roll made for the season, a blend of spiced meat with cranberries, a sort of pemmican in pastry.

A quick visit with Brian, known around here as Jam Daddy. Not an ad-lib musician, but an actual maker of jam. A crowd forms and I let him get back to his sweetening. Then I visit with Jesse, decked out in a seasonal sweater – red and green, aglitter with gold. She's next to a window, sun streaming through, where I have to squint in the gleam of her beacon-like top and find out where I can get one.

I move on to a trestle table of art by Nicola North, the painter who lives a short distance away. Her vibrant work grabs and holds me each time I see it. I choose a small print, one of her signature pieces – a stylized map of Vancouver Island, the outline of land with an encyclopedic representation of local flora and fauna in kaleidoscope colour.

Outside the barn, the low bumps of lavender fields have turned a soft crimson and emerald. Armed with purchases: artwork, nibbles, and gifts, we make our way back to the Gorge for another holiday market. Looping through Colwood and Langford, we see a man in a slicker stringing lights on a steep sloping roof. Nothing about it looks safe.

We follow Sooke Road past Hatley Park and Royal Roads University. A glimpse of open water, then the Gorge, sun glinting on watery oxbows. Clusters of mountain-ash berries dangle in festive red orange. Nature's decor. We enter Esquimalt Gorge Park and Pavilion, the parking lot already full, and we're directed to drive over the lip of the sidewalk and park on the walkway. On the water, outriggers glide by, now in bright sun, with paddlers in shirtsleeves. A bike wheels past with a long cart attached, its load a small girl and a tall Christmas tree. The girl gives us a regal wave, a princess in a parade.

We browse two storeys of crafters, the energy bustling, then drive to city centre, park the car, and continue on foot. James Bay Market has a Dickens theme now, a seasonal spin to its usual offerings, which happen from spring until fall. Now I'm zigging and zagging, sourcing the crux of each festive display through Victoria's downtown.

The Parkside Hotel is showcasing the Festive Tracks of Giving, a fundraiser for Rainbow Kitchen, a food security program. Their mandate: to facilitate food sharing and provide free hot meals to anyone in need. I learn more from Lisa and Mallory, part of the team coordinating the event. Their pride in the initiative is infectious. A model train's on display, a small Polar Express. Outside it's still sunny, but I pretend I'm a malamute and imagine the surroundings in snow.

From here I walk to the Hotel Grand Pacific, where a Gingerbread Showcase fills the lobby, part of Habitat for Humanity Victoria's fundraising drive for its Build Fund, spearheading affordable homeownership programs for local families. This year's theme is tradition, customs that bring us together, be it memories, holidays, relatives, or the families we choose. The public is welcome, donations encouraged. There's a stream of browsers and donors, the display of baked buildings impressive: a North Pole, an ice rink, a park. And perhaps the grandest construction, a replica of the hotel itself, making each gawker resemble a giant. I imagine us peering in windows, wondering if we might see tiny guests, maybe ticketholders for the miniscule train down the road.

On to the Royal BC Museum for WinterFest, an open-air market of tents and marquees encircling the museum's central building. Touted as a multicultural holiday market, at a glance it looks much like each craft fair I've seen, and yet each has its own personality – the space of the energy, traffic flow, a vibe from each vendor. Each one's appealing, but I'm aware of an intensity notching up as time passes. Perhaps the sense of a deadline, maybe sellers aware of bottom lines. The music is upbeat, the mood festive, but this feels more commercial than the fundraisers I've just come from.

Food trucks are parked around the museum's perimeter with a pop-up pub called the Snowman Tavern. Horses and carriages totter by, circling the Empress Hotel and the harbour. I take a few photos in sun and blue sky by a longhouse exhibit with totems, an extension of the museum's First Peoples Gallery, then turn toward the centre of town. Looking back, I do my best to interpret the vertical lineage shared in the poles. History, legend, and culture depicted in the tall painted carvings: Eagle, Wolf, Beaver, the Peoples. In this sunlight, the longhouse facade is catching sharp rays to illuminate one edge in a clean, distinct line, a timber cornerstone made of pure light.

Buses and coaches have vibrant regalia, bound for the Butchart Gardens. Festive dining and lights are now being featured, with carollers, a brass band, and a children's snowflake exhibit, all strung through the park's walkways, flower beds, hedges, and garlanded trees.

The story of Butchart is a good one, the vision of plant-lover and horticulturalist Jennie Butchart. After she moved from Ontario in 1904 with her husband Robert, the couple designed a cement plant for their new Island property to capitalize on limestone deposits surrounding Tod Inlet, on the west side of Saanich Peninsula near Brentwood Bay.

When the limestone supply was depleted, Jennie imagined refilling the space with a garden. A big one. Which she did by hand, hauling topsoil and earth with the aid of a cart and a horse, adding to her creation between 1906 and 1929. The recessed quarry was transformed into what's now the grand Sunken Garden display.

As the garden grew under Jennie's care, in a way it became global, with the addition of a Japanese Garden, an Italian Garden, and a Mediterranean Garden, along with a Rose Garden. Now a year-round tourist draw, the gardens also serve as an environmental initiative with ongoing research and development, a legacy Jennie would approve of.

Walking farther into the city, this being Lekwungen land of the Songhees and Esquimalt Nations, I see more signage for seasonal attractions. Hatley Castle at Royal Roads University is now decorated, with longer opening hours. Craigdarroch Castle, on a rise just behind me, is also adorned in seasonal finery, lit with bright wreaths and garland. And a short walk from here is Belfry Theatre, a restored 19th century church, now featuring *A Wonderheads Christmas Carol*, a unique spin on the Dickens tale.

Wonderheads, not to be confused with wonder-worker Saint Nick, is a "physical theatre company specializing in mask performance and visual storytelling." In this case, a full play with no spoken words, just evocative music and stage actors in outsize masks, each facial expression rich with emotion. With its music, stage lights, and effects, the performance is dreamy, almost ethereal, and an effective representation of Dickens's ghostly classic.

Back downtown at the Bay Centre mall, I admire the floors of lit trees, with central lights in a column of gold, two storeys of faux branches and wreaths, ornaments, baubles, more lights. You could get your fill of the festive season right here, assuming you prefer being indoors. Carols are playing, shoppers loaded with bags, and I can imagine the Grinch hating it here, that is, until his heart becomes grossly enlarged.

Outside, the sun's easing toward the water and I cross to Centennial Square, where the Lights of Wonder display is now on. The space is spectacular – illuminated white trees, sheen of metal, the look of earthbound constellations, an installation around steps of red brick. The Square will be busy at night, but I'm loving it in this afternoon twilight, the setting sun, lights waking up, as though I'm catching it all unawares.

Two cedar totems stand with the seasonal trees, where signage conveys a message of gratitude: *The Story of the Spirit Poles*. "We give thanks to the 'Two Brothers' (cedar trees) for allowing us to transform them into teachers that acknowledge the ability of Aboriginal Peoples to preserve and continue the cultural practices of their ancestors. We are proud that the City of Victoria has included the inherent keepers of Lekwungen Tung'uxw (Songhees Lands) in the transformation of this Square."

Along with the message is a kind of "table of contents," describing the story conveyed in each totem, which serves as a legend or crib sheet to eliminate uncertainty when reading the vertical history. From top to bottom on one pole: the Top Figure (Transformer), then Blankets of Salmon, Raven, and Xe'els (knowledge, teacher, creator), with a Mink design skirting the base. On the second pole, the Top Figure is Eagle, a human figure set within, then Wolf, followed by Otters, and finally Grandmother Moon. History, lineage, and culture captured in carvings of wood, similar to mask dances I've witnessed on other Pacific Coast islands, south and north of here. Imagery not unlike that of the Dickensian spin on the Wonderheads plays. Legends with lessons and morals conveyed through performance and art. Music and rhythm are part of the patter, dialogue not required. A few moments of contemplation, a few photos, and I'm off to another concert.

The venue is Victoria's Christ Church Cathedral. The event, *'Tis the Season*, a full choral show by the University of Victoria choir, this being their winter concert. Entry is by donation, the church bursting capacity, and we shuffle down one side of the nave, looking out on the chancel, where we join more attendees admiring the show from the wings.

The building itself is impressive, Gothic in style, BC's largest cathedral, part of the Anglican Church of Canada. Architect J.C.M. Keith won the right to design it, part of an international competition held in 1896. The nave we just came through, with its high vaulted ceiling, was the only thing here for a while, the rest being completed over the next 20 years, the church consecrated in 1929.

Now, for the winter choral event, the choir is a mix of students and faculty. Most are on risers facing the nave, but a second vocal group is behind us, upstairs in the choir loft, traditionally where call-and-answer-type hymns would be sung with the congregation. Today's vocals are sumptuous, acoustically flawless. But the whole thing's a far cry from the other seasonal shows I've attended. There's no levity here. It's a serious affair. No radio carols or pop songs. I was expecting a little more fun. The performance, however, is superb. Aurally beautiful, yet slightly oppressive. I applaud every number but question the selection of music. Maybe I'm not the right audience, and can't help but wonder what Andy Williams would make of it all.

SIMPLE HOLIDAY MIRACLES

It's now evening, and Deb and I are in new lodgings, a hotel near Victoria Harbour that feels like a comfy apartment. Dinner downstairs by a cozy gas fire. Candles on tables. A cocktail. Something with chicken for supper. Our server is apologetic, as they've been surprised by a last-minute corporate event in a conference room. Too many patrons and too few employees to serve them. We feel for the staff and no longer care how long dinner will take. The fire's still glowing. We have photos to enjoy. If there was a grandparent to drive home later it would feel just like being with family.

I do one more loop around the harbour on foot. Lights on the walkway and pier. Red and green bulbs in the streetlamps. The Empress Hotel now agleam, with the Legislative Building tinted by an underlit fountain – siren red, silver green, aqua blue – a government version of a Vegas casino.

In our room we hear the *clip-clop* of shod horses' hooves, carriages hauling sightseers through the past. Spoked carriage wheels are adorned in white lights, now glowing in the dark, the look of transport from *Tron*, if *Tron* were set in the 19th century.

Tucked in for the night, I have an elevated view of the city overlooking a sliver of harbour, a few midrise buildings, hotels, and the lavish dome of the legislature, currently topped in a festive red-and-green lid made of lights, a birdcage dressed for a gala.

Late in the night the city goes dark, nearly silent, save for an intermittent *click-click* emanating from somewhere. Maybe the fridge or a fan. It sounds like someone trying to enter the room. A bit disconcerting. Someone from the corporate party, perhaps. Too many eggnogs, trying each room with their key. Stagger, *click-click*, nope. Stagger, *click-click*, nope. (Only seven more floors to go.)

Morning breaks, but the only reason I know this is because of the time on a clock. Outside it's still dark, and now wet. There's a rainfall warning, with a weather advisory: *Elevated ocean water levels are expected, exceeding high astronomical tide. Low barometric pressure will combine with a period of high tide. Minor coastal flooding is possible along exposed shorelines. Threat from wind and waves accompanying high water levels.*

Outside, my rain jacket's not keeping up, my sweater and shirt slowly soaking up rain as I crisscross some streets, and shiver. The weather's a swirl; wind and rain, with squalls off the harbour – a nautical, maritime day.

Around the waterfront, more streetlamps in red and green bulbs, a feeling of strolling through slim and neat yuletide trees. A few moored boats have their masts lit up too, with some hulls decorated as well. Purples and whites, ivory and cream, a few reds with the greens. The water's reflecting the glow, along with the lamps and the traffic lights. Everything feels especially festive.

I spot a fabulous carving display by Karl Morgan of the Tsawwassen First Nation. A bald eagle, white tail and head, taking two salmon, one red and one green. Not only symbolic but spiritual. Seasonal too. Maybe I'm overly aware of those classic red and green colours right now. Even last night, in the dark, getting oriented in a new space, I used the old trick of a few extra blinks. Which can help the retina adjust between rod cells and cones, our night-vision receptors and colour-detectors seeking out red, green, and blue.

Following the harbourside, we watch a floatplane putter out of the inlet. A ferry, Washington bound, sits silent, a whale awaiting a feeding of passengers. We duck into a café for coffee, where we settle into deep squishy chairs. The venue is set below street level, and I look *up* through a window at damp grassy ground, Victoria Harbour beyond. Then a traipse through a hotel lobby, still vibrantly lit in the dawn, but with the silence of "in-between" time, a caesura between musical bars. I can almost hear the harbour's sea lung inhaling, deep and meditative on the breadth of the bay.

Ads are posted for Feed the Need, collecting groceries and donations for food banks. The rain eases up, slightly, and we plan to explore further by car. But before we leave Victoria's downtown, I visit with Polina in the hotel lobby, her dialect strong and pronounced.

"Where's home for you, originally?" I ask.

She smiles. "Can you guess?"

"Ukraine."

Her face lights up. "Yes!"

"And where did you live in the country?"

"Zaporizhzhia," she says, meeting my gaze. "Where the bombing began. Not far from the nuclear plant."

"And your family?" I ask, flashing back to visits with Sasha in Summerland, that bridge of seasons spent in the Okanagan.

"Surviving," she adds, with a hint of flint in her eyes. "What can you do?" Then she smiles. "*Thank you*, Canada. Giving me a place, and a home. Where are you from?" she asks.

I tell her part-time Island, part-time mainland, Vancouver.

"Ah, your Stanley Park, so beautiful!" Her expression, I believe, much like mine when Doug lit up the Polar Express.

Then I ask about the festive season, what it's like for her.

"Well, 7th of January, 14 dishes on the table, every one of them different," she says, referring to Ukrainian tradition linked to the Julian calendar. Christmas Eve is January 6th, with celebrations continuing until January 19th, consistent with the Orthodox Church.

Many parishes, however, have shifted these dates to coincide with the Gregorian calendar, celebrating the festive season from December 24th until January 6th. Which is what my family would do with my mom's parents, the grandparents I knew as Baba and Dido. Celebrate in December, consistent with retail hours, then have another big feast and more presents to finish the season with a nod to the past, on January 6th. Often my birthday, in the first week of January, would join in the mix, for an intense fortnight of eating and repurposing gift wrap.

I admit to Polina I'd forgotten about the set courses of food, one dish for each day of the two-week occasion. Although many Ukrainians I know have a roster of 12 dishes: cooked wheat with honey, beet borscht, meaty gravy, perogies, cabbage rolls, herring, cooked mushrooms, braided bread washed in egg, stewed cabbage, cooked beans, fried donut-like buns, and a fruit soup or compote to finish. Often we'd have plum-filled perogies, a blend of savoury-sweet. Then we'd retire to the sofa or floor to digest and fart, though not always in that order.

It's time to move on but I feel, maybe along with Polina, that we've both met a kind of relation. Simple holiday miracles, tradition and custom in places that may not be your first, nor your last, destination. ❖

Faux Snow, Ferry Style

Overleaf: Ferry from Swartz Bay by Galiano and Mayne Islands

Late Season Fishing, South Island

Arrival of the 'Reindeer' in Horseshoe Bay,
Chemainus Mural by Sandy Clark and Lea Goward

AT CHEMAINUS

It's a Wonderful Life Radio Play, Chemainus Theatre

Skating on Fuller Lake, Chemainus Mural by Dan Sawatzky

Overleaf: Decorations around Duncan

RAINBOWS AND SONGBIRDS IN FLOCKS

From Victoria we drive up the Saanich Peninsula, through farmland and forest. Ducks paddle on fields in fallow, the ground flooded with pools of old rain while new showers slant from the east. Near the top of the peninsula we exit to Sidney, where the sea sprays in gusts, leaping across the road from the beach. *Elevated ocean levels expected.* More swirling weather, a few rays of sun, then a rainbow bursts into view as songbirds dive through the colourful arc.

I take two days "off" from my festive excursions, catch up on mail and watch TV, a seasonal feel with sitcom reruns of holiday specials: office parties on *The Office*, *Seinfeld*'s "Festivus," *30 Rock* celebrating "Ludachristmas," and the "Holiday Armadillo" sharing Hannukah lessons on *Friends*. All of which trigger memories from this time of year. A favourite of mine is one I've previously shared (in more than one book) but feel an obligation to share once again. Regifting, if you like.

It was well into December, not quite school holidays. I was ten or eleven at the time. There was a festive bowl of unshelled nuts on the table, laid out with a nutcracker: Brazil nuts and filberts, walnuts, pecans, and almonds, plus a black box of Pot of Gold chocolates. With Mandarin oranges as well, their perforated cardboard container like tiny portholes to a much wider world.

Dad was in his comfy chair, facing the TV from across the room. And he asked me to toss him an orange. So I chose a good plump one, removed its crinkly green tissue, and lobbed it in his direction, same as when we played slow-pitch. At that precise moment, however, something on TV caught his attention, an ad for a holiday special, and he was focused on the screen rather than the orange missile sailing toward him.

I had time to holler out, "Dad!" I believe, or that may've just been in my mind. All I know is the big juicy orange dropped squarely into his crotch with a soft, fleshy *thud*.

Poor Dad folded neatly in two, inadvertently doing an elevated ab-crunch, his head tucking between his knees as he let out a yelp like the time the neighbour's dog caught its tail in a door.

"Ouch," said my sister, looking at Dad, still folded in half.

"Oh my," added Mom, her tone one of genuine concern.

"Sorry, Dad," was all I could muster.

He took a great deal of time to catch his breath, then he wheezed, "Oh, son, you got me right in the..." And he said a word I'd never heard before.

Next day at school, I was discussing it with male friends on the playground.

"You know what my dad calls them?" I asked. The boys shook their heads, leaning in, eager to acquire worldly knowledge. I puffed my chest, delighted to be the one in the know.

"Tentacles!" I said loudly, proud to share a new term for our anatomical nether regions. Everyone seemed impressed. Sex education, by the way, was not in our curriculum.

"Say," a boy named Scott piped up. "Isn't that what octopuses have?"

"Uh, yeah," I said, uncertain, but I soldiered on. "All I know is it's another name for gonads. My dad said so."

The rest of the group nodded slowly, realizing we'd all learned something invaluable. We also knew if it came from a parent, it had to be true. It was a very long time before it occurred to me I might have misheard Dad, though I'm still not convinced that I did. ❖

IMMERSED IN THE SEASON

Present day, solo again, and I'm back on the road, exploring the Island, immersed in the season. I stop at a diner, where I visit with Kellie, whose family goes back a long way around here. Specifically, Cobble Hill, between Saanich Inlet and Shawnigan Lake. And I ask her about the region.

"Well, our uncle Jack owned most of this land. Donated a lot of it too. What's now a park. He built the first suspension bridge. A small one, but it was the first river-crossing around here." She smiles, remembering. "Even after we moved to the mainland, we came here for summers. I spend Christmas here too. Nine kids, with plenty of cousins. We'll have about 30 sitting down to holiday dinner. Everyone draws an envelope, early in the season, so we all have something to do, something to bring. We each put a little money in too. Then we rent dishes, cutlery, tablecloths, and no one needs to do cleanup. It's big, but pretty easy as well."

Neatly enough, Andy Williams is crooning from a sound system. "O Holy Night."

"Jack passed away quite a few years ago," Kellie adds, nodding slowly. "And he was eclectic. Like, *really* eclectic."

I smile. "Now you have to tell me."

"Well, he'd been diagnosed with bone cancer, but he said he was okay with it. Really. Understood his time would be over soon. So he built his own coffin. Out in the garage."

I sip my coffee, thinking that through. "What else?" I ask.

"Oh, you'd never just walk onto the property, not without calling ahead. He kept the place booby-trapped. You know, things that could really hurt a person. But he was a good man. Completely self-reliant."

"Give me an example."

"Okay, one time, we went over. We were visiting with Auntie Mabel, 'cause we thought Jack was napping. He was using a walker by then. Until we realized he was up on the roof, fixing something. How he got up there we'll never know, or how he got down. There were plenty of people around; he could've called them to give him a hand, but that wasn't his way."

Funnily, I thought of those mythic stories people convey about finding an infant on a high bookcase or mantel, before the child can walk, with no visible means of access. Leaving us to wonder if perhaps we can levitate, even fly, until others convince us we can't.

On the stereo, Andy hits his final high note as the Vince Guaraldi Trio takes over. "Skating" from *A Charlie Brown Christmas*.

"Have you been to Ladysmith, for the lights?" Kellie asks.

I tell her I have.

"Did you see Pamela Anderson's place? It's right by the highway. That was her grandma's property, I believe."

I know of the place but haven't gone looking.

"Have you tried the local wines?" Kellie asks. "Beautiful vineyards around here. And teas. Did you know that?"

I say I had no idea.

"Yeah, wonderful teas. They're all green you know, taken when the plants are still growing."

I make a note to find some, but for now simply finish my coffee.

"Oh," Kellie adds, "have you done the West Coast Trail?"

I admit that I haven't, only the trailheads on the west side of the Island.

"We did it as a class, Community Rec, in high school," she says. "Had a wonderful teacher, Mr. Shore. We *made* our canoes. Two of them. Molded the fibreglass. Everything. This was in Nanaimo. Then we made our way out to the trail, with our two new canoes. Took turns portaging. Ten days of hiking. Our teacher carried only ten pounds in his pack. Lived off the land. Taught us so many things. I tracked him down, years later, to thank him. What a difference he made. One of those teachers, you know? Really good."

She points at a painting adorning a wall, a sea view through pines. "See that? That's what we looked at, every night when we camped on the trail. Just spectacular." She looks at the painting. Another smile. "I gotta say, I was awfully lucky. Having a teacher like that. Living here and experiencing that." A sigh. "Well, time to go. Safe travels!" And she waves as we go separate ways. ❁

A SENSE OF BELONGING

The radio's off and all I can hear is the soft, gritty spin of the tires, the road now sanded and salted. The conversation with Kellie conjures memories of exploring the Pacific side of the Island with Deb. From Victoria, west into Sooke, through Shirley to Port Renfrew and beyond. I remember coming through, west-Island bound, imagining this as a kind of salt path, a trek like a pilgrimage trail. I'd just finished reading Raynor Winn's *The Salt Path*, her memoir leaving its own saline residue.

In keeping with that, we visited a local salt works just outside Sooke, making our way along Highway 14, the south of Vancouver Island a snaggle of inlets and blunt-edged peninsulas. East Sooke Regional Park covers much of the southernmost coast, with trails through forest and a shoreline of treed skerries. From Sooke we drove to Saltwest Naturals and met Jeff, who owns and runs the business with Jess. One of those unique businesses that's both modern and ancient. A wood structure serves as a shop, with manufacturing out back, the process seemingly simple but requiring the nuance and intricacies of winemaking.

Clear, local seawater is pumped into solar greenhouses where a combination of sun and wind are used to create handcrafted batches of sundried sea salt. From there, different seasonings are added to the crystalline flakes to make organically infused gourmet salts. We bought packets of flor-de-sal, plus salt blended with rosemary, sage, and sweet-smoky maple. By sprinkling a selection of these onto food I was able to create a visually festive dusting of green, red, and white. The subtle sweet-savoury mix, too, was effective.

Sticking to the coast-hugging highway, we stopped in the forest where patio umbrellas drew us to Shirley Delicious for lunch: homemade soup with bakery sandwiches in the town that's also named Shirley. Carrying on west with a northerly lilt, we passed French Beach Provincial Park, eventually veering from the coast to skirt the inlet at Port Renfrew. The yawn of sea creating this dent is Port San Juan. Botanical Beach Provincial Park sits like a toe on the foot of the land while across the inlet Carmanah Walbran Provincial Park sprawls up the Island's west coast, eventually joining Pacific Rim National Park Reserve, Barkley Sound, and the smear of islets known as the Broken Group.

The bay here enters the Strait of Juan de Fuca, the southern part of the Salish Sea, and from this point opens up to the Pacific. The Canada–US border cuts through the middle of the strait, with Washington's Olympic Peninsula due south. This bit of water sits at the centre of what's known as the Graveyard of the Pacific, the treacherous length of coast that runs from the Columbia Bar in Oregon to the northern tip of Vancouver Island. From the early 19th century to the start of the 20th century, over 130 ships foundered here.

This is Pacheedaht land, part of the Nuu-chah-nulth Nations, *Pacheedaht* translating to "people of the sea foam." With this water's history of swallowing ships, I could imagine ravenous spindrift and sea billows gnawing the shoals. As Europeans arrived, this became another centre for fishing and forestry. Port Renfrew was dubbed *Tall Tree Capital of Canada*, something I found unsurprising. Steep conifer-draped slopes face the inlet, the land itself serving as a logging accessory, gravity enabling cutters to fell trees that would tumble toward the water, aiding the shifting and dragging of timber into booms and to mills.

To break up the drive, Deb and I hiked a trail on old logging land. A short distance from the path, in a knot of saplings and ferns, sat the rusty remains of a donkey engine, peering from undergrowth as though hiding. These steam-powered winches were used to drag freshly felled timber to the next stage of transport and milling.

With resource industry having taken a backseat to tourism, the inlet of Port San Juan is now a primary access point for anglers, birders, kayakers, and hikers. This is the junction of the West Coast and Juan de Fuca Trails, where Kellie and her classmates transported their handmade canoes to begin the journey northwest from here. It's also prime real estate for sea lion and whale watching, with top billing going to orcas.

My first up-close-and-personal encounter with orcas, however, took place on the opposite edge of the Island, a geographical one-eighty to the northeast. I was launching a kayak when three big transient whales cut though the shallows, dorsal fins two metres high. If I'd been fly casting, I could've touched them with my leader and fly. The feeling was unlike anything I'd experienced. Something about being partially submerged in the water created an intense connection, a link to living geography, belonging, right then and there.

One of the orcas leapt at that moment, a thundering breach that made its own waves, shoving the kayak against my legs. The pod exhaled in unison, a roll of sea lungs – *pffooo, pffooo, pffooo* – as they glided away, their wake a pulse of vibration. ❖

WHERE RAINFOREST GREETS SEA

My plan was to complete more of an Island circumference, to venture up the west coast, north of Port Renfrew, to Ucluelet and Tofino. The draw for me was the festive event known as the Hundred Voice Choir, a holiday choral celebration featuring, as locals put it, "100 Tofitians and Ucluetians singing in harmony on the beautiful west coast of Vancouver Island." Which sounds ideal: storm season for watching big ocean water, along with another relaxed sharing of seasonal song. What could be better? So I reach out to Karen, one of the organizers, to track down some tickets.

"Sorry," she explains in an email. "No can do."

At first I think I've waited too late, like the full train bookings in Duncan. But no. The choral director has suffered a concussion, resulting in the concert being cancelled this time around. Word has it the director is all right and recovering nicely. I'll just have to wait for the singing ensemble to reconvene, and plan to return in the future.

The Tofino Resort and Marina, however, is featuring its Sea of Lights, a waterborne light-up much like a parade, but the floats here *actually* float. Boats with seasonal lights strung on rigging and masts, gunwales and hulls decked in holiday hues. Another fine-sounding affair, but I'd rather not drive our vehicle over the central hump of the Island in winter conditions. Our car's a fair-weather ride.

So I look for alternate transport: a bus or a floatplane, even a small private flight, but nothing is running at this time of year, everything geared toward the busier months from spring until fall. For now I need to be content with memories from previous treks, when days were longer and warmer. Although the last time Deb and I came to this side of the Island, to explore around Port Renfrew, it was already autumn. We stayed a few sleepy nights in a self-contained rental, a bed and breakfast without any breakfast. The power went out every day. A vacation of flashlights and candles, board games and books. What felt like old-fashioned fun. The little structure that housed us sat atop a sheer cliff with views of inlet and pine, tagged by locals as *the place where rainforest meets sea*. Which I viewed as a natural greeting, as though water and trees were embracing.

We were barely an hour by car from the Island's busy south end, but it felt like a lifetime away. The jagged inlet resembles a fjord, a spit pointing at sea, a breakwater curve, the narrows a brackish mingle of saltwater and fresh as a river flows into the ocean. From a main road, we followed the water inland, heading north, to a roughly kept park, a place of coarse granite, rock-climbing, and natural pools in jade green. Even late in the season, swimmers plunged in the ponds, water rippling to aquamarine. The thought of it still makes me shiver.

The town of Port Renfrew fronts the river, inlet, and sea, and it was here that I touched the two coastal path trailheads: the West Coast Trail and the Juan de Fuca Marine Trail, which head in opposite directions, roughly speaking, northwest and southeast. For those ambitious enough to attempt it, completing either of these trails must feel remarkable, a rugged week-long accomplishment.

I remember other friends describing their completion of the West Coast Trail, as a family, over a week – mom, dad, and two teenage daughters. Not an outdoorsy group, but they borrowed gear and did the trip as a team, navigating ladders, wet logs and damp tents. Seven days of dried food was a bore, they explained, not to mention being covered in mud. But it became an excursion in strength, perseverance, endurance, something none of them thought possible, not on their own, yet together they were successful. When they told me about it, much later, their delight filled a very large room.

In Sooke, you can pick up the Galloping Goose Regional Trail. This is part of the Trans Canada, or Great Trail – roadways, greenways, and waterways joining the Pacific, Atlantic, and Arctic Oceans – the longest recreational, multi-use trail in the world. It was this vast network of trails that I followed elsewhere on Vancouver Island, as well as through BC's lower mainland and into the Okanagan.

As we toured the southwest of the Island, Deb and I spent a night in a seaside cottage outside of Sooke, where we woke to a day of grey mizzle. The sun wanted to shine, I believe, but a quilt of water-soaked cloud had other plans. So in lieu of a hike we drove to Sheringham Distillery, where the company melds their own story with local lore.

One of the original founders lived in a cabin near Sheringham Point, where he discovered moonshine bottles from the town's old hotel, a 1930s establishment "with a Wild West reputation." The hotel burned down in the 1980s but its legend survives. At a creek near the cabin, former prospectors worked a long sluice box, panning for gold. Following a good year, the miners would come into town and buy enough whisky to supply the entire community for festive celebrations lasting from Christmas until New Year's Day.

Sheringham Distillery started in Shirley, which was where we returned to sample their gins. Since then, the business has grown and moved into Langford.

But on that overcast day, we had a view of the headland and coast, where the Sheringham Point Lighthouse still stands. Gazing at the water from the distillery, I thought of the history of liquor around here. This was an active rum-running route in the 1920s and '30s. Prohibition had ended in Canada but continued in the United States until 1933. And while exporting liquor from Canada was legal, importing it to the US was not. Boats would leave here, north of the border, loaded with liquor, compliant with regulations, morphing to lawbreaking smugglers the moment they crossed the strait, where most made their way to sheltered coves on Washington's Olympic Peninsula.

When we visited, the distillery had a small parking lot, and I had to wedge the vehicle next to a phone pole. Inside the shop, I found a bottle of gin that I felt would pair nicely with anything. Pleased with my purchase, I was thinking about mixers when I started the car and backed up, forgetting about the phone pole. Then I heard a horrible *scrunch* as I sheared off the driver's side mirror, leaving it dangling from a long knot of wires like a nightmarish teddy bear eye. I blurted five of the seven words George Carlin said you can't say on TV, then secured the mirror with a clump of red duct tape that I had in the trunk. So long as I slouched and leaned to the left, the mirror worked reasonably well, tiding us over until I got it repaired, which I eventually did. I then did the math. All-in cost of my bottle of gin: $600. ✿

Winter Market, Bilston Creek Farm, Victoria

Lavender Field, Bilston Creek Farm

Late Apples at Bilston Creek Farm

Festive Berries, North Island

Overleaf: Poinsettia, Campbell River

Holiday Shopping aboard the Ferry

Mitten Ornament, Nanaimo Christmas Market

A FESTIVE MYSTERY

Driving north, having left the lower half of the Island for now, I'm once more on my own while Deb's on the mainland. Presently, I'm outside Nanaimo, making my way toward Parksville, bound for Comox and Courtenay, to experience as much of the season as possible. Stopping to fill up the tank, I visit with Peter, who's wearing a puffy jacket with a blue ribbon looped on his chest. I thought I knew every iteration of statement, public appeal, awareness, but this declaration is new to me, and I ask him what the blue ribbon means.

"Free the hostages from Gaza," he says. Eye contact, a thin smile, and a nod.

"Ah," I say, understanding, I believe, the layers that accompany that. And I consider my friendship with Khaled, and new friends from this trip, Randa, Rabbi Bentzi, and Blumie, as my mind shifts to festivals and lights, overlapping beliefs, and familial traits. All of it shared.

I smile and wish Peter safe travels, and he does the very same thing.

Our interaction hangs in my mind as I pass a sign warning drivers, of what I'm unsure. Cautions of things up ahead, risks we can't simply ignore

Another sign, a yellow diamond, warns of low-flying aircraft. I'm compelled to look up, waiting for a plane to buzz over the passing lane. No planes, mind you, but three geese fly by in a compact formation, snowy white. (Snow geese?) As they pass, I can see only one, so perfect and tight is their flight, drafting like cyclists in wind, the precision of fighter-jet pilots.

Today is light sky over low, heavy cloud. An inversion. Mountaintops clearly defined while the coastline is shrouded in fog. The sea looks like foil reused, wrinkled and partially flattened. Clouds in slashes, an unfinished tic-tac-toe match. The next sign indicates where I'm heading: *Cumberland, Courtenay, Comox*. Another sea glimpse, steely water under patchy blue sky.

Now a sign for Parksville and Port Alberni. Leaving the highway, I follow the Oceanside Route into Parksville. The town motto, *Live, Work, Play*. I stop at Parksville Museum, park the car next to cypress, some roses, and long slender cedars, then visit with Linda, who works here.

"How's the season?" I ask.

"Oh, it gets quiet here. The snowbirds, they start arriving."

"Snowbirds?" I say. "From where?" Unsure if we're talking about people or geese.

Linda assures me it's people, indicating where they're all from. "Alberta, Saskatchewan, Ontario. Come for two to six months, now through the winter."

"I thought the locals go south," I say. "Places like Yuma, in Arizona."

"Oh, no. They know what they're doing, coming here. The museum will be quiet, though. We close between Christmas and New Year's." She smiles. "I don't mind. But enjoy yourself, take a look around. Let me know if you have any questions."

Church bells ring from the museum grounds and I think of Shane MacGowan's festive song, his lyrics of bells ringing out. The tolling, mind you, truncates our visit, as though I'm subtly being encouraged to move on. I smile and nod, wish Linda well, and walk through a door into history.

Outside is a short nature walk, a trail through beech trees and birch. An informative board describes what I might find in here: huckleberries, salal, a rust-coloured flicker or two. Beyond the "Nature Break" trail, a path curves through a preserved settlers' village. Buildings date to the late 19th century: a post office and house in log-framed construction, more structures in planks, a blacksmith, firehall, tractor barn, and Knox United Church. Could that be where the bells were ringing?

It's unlikely, as no one else is around, their echo one more unsolved mystery.

By the main pavilion is a placard, a landscape photo of the shore beyond the trees, something from the past. It could be Rathtrevor Beach as it was, before campsites. The sign reads *Gilakas'la*, a traditional welcome commonly used in the language of the Kwakwa̱ka̱'wakw People. This, mind you, is Snaw-naw-as, Coast Salish land. The greeting translates to, "I share my breath and spirit with yours." Phraseology I associate with a Māori *hongi*, the pressing of foreheads and noses, acknowledging shared spirit and space. Or the Hindi *namaskar*, which can indicate, "I'll see you in that place we're all one."

The sign also features the artwork of Coast Salish artist Joe Bob, a rendering of two carved paddles, reminding me of the paddlers we watched slicing their way through the Gorge in Esquimalt. Bob's depictions have the clean vibrant lines of traditional Salish design in red, white, and black. With an additional swath of deep blue, a lapis tone like deepwater sea.

For a settler museum there's a representative balance that fits with the land. That and the small nature trail. I like it here throughout the year but love it right now. Chill and damp, quiet and utterly private. I do my best to soak up the space, retain this window to elsewhere, or more accurately, another time. Then shuffle back to the car, still heading north.

At Riptide Lagoon, a sign reads *See You in March!* A painted sand dollar points toward Rathtrevor Park, and another is advertising holiday wreaths. I cross a steely orange bridge spanning Englishman River, pushing me on with a jostle.

I do a loop around Parksville, admire the hand-cut wood construction of St. Anne's Anglican Church, constructed in 1894. Another trail winds through the forest, where locals have decorated the path, little houses like art drops with gnomes, birdhouses, shiny baubles, and stars. It looks like a festive display, but it's like this year-round, a splash of whimsy just off the highway.

At a bookstore in the centre of town I visit with Jeannie, her lineage a historic mosaic, Indigenous and ginger-haired settlers.

"What's this season mean to you?" I ask.

She doesn't need time to answer. "Family. And, well, really, it's about dinner. Sitting around, together, and eating. I mean, gifts are nice but not that important. We have family come down from Royston and Courtenay. Sometimes as many as 18 jammed in our little place." She smiles, and I can tell that she loves it. Then adds, "We're not religious, you know. The church beat *that* out of us, back when we were kids."

She gives me a hug, like a shared understanding, and I bustle out before getting emotional. From the car I spy Mount Arrowsmith, today merely shoulders disappearing in cloud. The next sign on the road reads, *Qualicum Beach, Port Alberni, Campbell River.* I pass a field of old hay, cut but unstacked, lying flaccid and flaxen. The sign after that indicates *Highway 4, Pacific Rim National Park Reserve, Bamfield, Ucluelet, and Tofino,* where I hope the concussed convalescing conductor is still doing well.

TICKLING THE HEART OF THE ISLAND

After checking weather and road conditions, I won't venture west at this time, here in the midst of the Island. Too much elevation involved, which I can't tackle safely, so again I'll reflect on an earlier season, when I explored this part of the region.

If I were to launch myself for an aerial view, I'd see that Vancouver Island is shaped like a giant canoe, waiting, perhaps, to be propelled by paddles like those painted by Joe Bob. The Island "boat" is about 450 kilometres from bow to stern, and 100 kilometres wide at the beam. To complete the imagery, the craft's bearing northwest, with Port Alberni being on a geographical thwart, two-thirds of the way back from the prow, where a paddler might sit to steer.

I take out my Nicola North painting, study it like a photo, her interpretative map of this evergreen boat. Only now do I realize, perhaps, why I chose this piece at this time. The colours, earthen and rich, nudge into the festive, a palette of forest green with late-season crimson: berries and mushrooms and delicate petals. There's a dogwood, an acorn, blackberries, salal, a bee busy at work, with a leaf of the ubiquitous Garry Oak near the base of the Island, as though giving shade to the provincial capital at the stern of this craft.

Which gets me thinking about mapmaking in general, artistry and the interpretation of terrain. North's art reminds me of some of the world's earliest atlases, when maps conveyed more than topography. Storytelling in a manner, cartographers relaying tales through illumination and symbols, graphic painting that might warn of sea beasts or dragons. Not merely directions but guidelines, cautions, reminders. A whole other take on "Lookout Ahead."

With that notion of true exploration and discovery, I flash back to a previous trip round the thwart of this big Island boat, aiming toward the Pacific. The day was sunny and warm, the drive a series of sharp climbs and curves. Technically, I'd hit the west coast, but it's actually closer to the middle of the Island, with Alberni Inlet reaching far inland, a lengthy blue arm tickling the heart of the Island.

It was midmorning, a weekday, but each time I drive this stretch of road I'm surprised by the volume of traffic. Passenger vehicles, commercial haulers, the road shuttling people and industry. But with no deadlines the drive was relaxed and enjoyable, the road undulating and weaving, conducive to loud music and singing at volume. I remember listening to one of the local stations, when an ad came on for a business hiring swampers.

Musically, "swampers" was a name given to session players from Alabama who recorded with Aretha Franklin and others. But around here, as in other maritime centres, swampers are boat captain's assistants. Which I found fun, knowing they're still in demand, as that's exactly what I'm supposed to be when I grow up. This was determined when I was a student in junior high school and we took career aptitude tests, a 20-minute quiz to determine how to spend the rest of our lives.

My test results indicated I should be part of a boat captain's crew, which I found rather cool. Not exactly the Viking life I'd envisioned, but not too far from it. The only obstacle to my becoming part of a boat crew, however, was the fact there were no boats to crew on Okanagan Lake, the Interior Salish land where I grew up. Just ski boats, sailboats, and canoes, and a weed-threshing contraption that patrolled the lake's perimeter, hacking out hairy green hunks of Eurasian watermilfoil, and *that* ugly vessel in puce wasn't hiring. However, when the waterborne weed-whacking craft proved ineffective, shrimp were released into the water in the hopes that they'd eat the lake clean of weeds. But of course, they just messed with the ecosystem, decimating everything else – like introducing rabbits and goats. Not as you would at a cocktail party, you understand.

"Rabbit, meet goat."

"Goat, this is rabbit."

Not like that, but rather the shrimp were introduced to the habitat, and like rabbits and goats elsewhere, became invasive, decimating the native species that already lived there. So when the shrimp proved to be more of a bother than a benefit, for a short period of time a shrimping boat trundled around the lake, trying to remove what had only recently been dumped there.

That was the moment when I felt I had a shot at getting hired as a swamper, part of a proper boat crew in my mostly landlocked hometown. I never did hear back from the city, however, town council being the ones that ran the shrimp boat. But in their defence, my resume at the time was spartan. *Education: Grade 9. Experience: Grade 9. Special Skills: Acne.* But I liked to believe that maybe, one day, I could be a real-life swamper. If not on a boat, then perhaps as an R & B session player like the ones Aretha Franklin employed. So of course I wanted to pull over, update my resume and send it in to the station. I'd just need to change Career Objective from *Viking* to *Swamper.* However, turns out the employer *did* end up hiring mariners from a range of backgrounds, forcing me to shelve my swamper dreams once again.

On that particular westerly drive it was autumn, but with enough reds and greens, tinted leaves among evergreen needles, that it already felt rather festive. I remember the day turning a corner, as though finally deciding how to proceed. Cloud moved on, leaving a sky of clear blue. I pulled off Highway 4 by Cameron Lake, its rippled surface the same hue as the sky. I had a fishing rod, a small box of tackle, and some food to serve as a picnic. And I hiked through foliage to the lakeside. Gravel scrunched underfoot as I looked for a break in the greenery. Here the roadway borders low cliffs, a scramble of glacial rock, with a fence-like mesh of brambles, blackberry barbs, chokecherry, and willowy willows.

Forcing my way, I found footing on rocks, navigating between fallen logs. The thicket opened slightly, creating a quasi-cave of leaf, branch, and bark, a three-metre bubble in the tangle of foliage. The compact green hollow fronted the shore, the lake deep and cold, where I imagined a few hungry trout within casting range. With a satisfied smile I unpacked my kit: reel with monofilament line, rod in five sections, and a tiny container of lures with flies in compartmented rows. Kicking off my shoes, I waded into the water, shuffling on sand and rock to gain purchase, toes behaving like fingers. And with a wiggle of ankles and turn of the hips, I secured myself, a batter digging in at home plate.

A few casts, feeling the breeze, a light chop on the water. And then, 20 metres away, a naked man stepped from the brush, a Rastafarian sasquatch, to saunter into the lake, where he stood knee-high in the water, then turned and raised his chin at me.

"S'up?" said the hairy nude man.

"Alright?" I said, raising my chin in reply, then cast the opposite way, deciding the sausage I'd packed for a snack had lost its appeal.

The dreadlocked sasquatch didn't last long in the chill of the lake, and within a few minutes I had my fishing nook back to myself – my fully clothed, civilized self.

It didn't take long for me to give up on fishing as well, and I carried on in the car, driving westward, deeper into the forest. Behind me, the lake glinted in sapphire shades, then I pulled off the highway again. This time at MacMillan Provincial Park, part of the coastal western hemlock biogeoclimatic zone, home to the largest and oldest western red cedar and Douglas fir trees around here, some 900 years old. There's a trailhead on both sides of the highway, and although the speed limit drops and there's a lighted pedestrian crossing, people still dash across the blind curve of road like spooked animals, risking their lives.

On my side of the road, stepping out of the vehicle, I was immediately ensconced in old growth.

Just south of here is Kuth-kah-chulth, one of several commanding peaks surrounding Mount Arrowsmith Massif Regional Park. A blend of energy hangs in the forest, whimsical and yet staunchly ancient as well. Perhaps the trees' venerability adds a ponderous feeling, maybe the weight of the world. But along with that meditative mood, a sense of play resonates. Remarkably, no traffic went by and I had the forest to myself for several minutes, which felt awfully close to eternity, plunked in the world's grandest yule tree lot.

The south side of the park is home to the largest Douglas firs, while the northern forest boasts more cedars, the stands abutting the lake where I fished with the sasquatch. I lingered among the trees for a while, the deep-ridged bark of the firs like wrinkles in elephant skin, laugh lines and furrowing brows. Flowering lichen commonly known as "old man's beard" covered low-hanging branches, dangling like wispy green bunting, as though the path through the trees might lead to a joust or medieval fete. Or perhaps further back, older still, to an ancient and seasonal harvest, a Wild Hunt led by a god.

The chortle of a big rig shifting down, applying the Jake brake, pulled me back to the present. I made my way back to the car, and as a slipstream of traffic finally passed, I carried on to a hole in the wall. Literally. At a notch in the road, with a little finagling, I turned the vehicle around to park by a path descending to a thicket of trees in a shallow valley. A few hundred metres into the woods I was on proper trail – tree roots, dirt, mud. The trail was well-used, decorated in scraps of litter. A toddler's pants lay on the ground, discarded. As well as a single sport sock, a new home to a large dripping slug, snuggling into the cotton. Banana slug, I believe, the same kind I stepped on in a previous journey, to my surprise and mild revulsion. Both of us, it should be noted, were unharmed.

The path sloped down in a steady trajectory for about a kilometre, then I heard a trickle of water along with some voices. A handful of people were there, clambering on the edge of a slow-moving creek, taking selfies. Two women were giggling. They'd gotten themselves into a predicament, having shimmied along a deadfall over the water to get a good shot. By the time I arrived they seemed stuck, trying to determine how to get down.

"All good?" I asked.

"I think so," one of the two said with a laugh. "Just questioning our choices."

I wished them well and climbed down to the water to take my own set of pictures. What I photographed is the Hole in the Wall, an embankment of rock and clay sharply sheered into vertical sides, creating a freestanding wall of muddy stone. A circular hole is chiselled through the centre of the natural earthwork, about two metres diameter. A pipeline used to pass through the embankment, and a number of years ago the pipe was removed but the hole remains, now a tidy round culvert of earth where a side stream feeds into a creek.

A few sightseers were sloshing through the water and into the culvert. Wanting, I suppose, a photo looking back to where I was standing, along with a few other people. This resulted in long awkward pauses as everyone waited for everyone else to get out of their shot. Which never happened. So people gave up, instead taking pictures of strangers from a distance, all looking into their cameras impatiently.

A tourist brochure describes this spot as "a beautiful oasis in the forest where the creek flows through the hole and down into the crystal-clear pool below." Which is accurate, but what I found most alluring about this pocket of treed creek were the dozens of inuksuit, or inukshuks – fist-sized river rocks neatly stacked into towers and humanoid shapes – a procession of little stone people fording the river. At a glance they could pass for stony snowmen out of season, wading through shallows in search of cold weather or a holiday card. Not unlike the festive Wonderheads, music performed without dialogue, the effect surreal, adding a dreaminess that somehow kept the present at bay. In its way, conjuring spirits, those past and those yet to arrive.

AN ALMOST REVERENTIAL HUSH

Having explored the Hole in the Wall, I was back in the car, continuing west through the valley, on to a sleepy community, crossing numbered avenues with a gradual descent to town centre. Following my nose, I made a couple of turns, ending up on what felt like a main street. I was amazed by the vastness of space, a community built when land was plentiful. Quiet four-lane streets in addition to angled parking. Shopfronts across the street from each other seemed hundreds of metres apart. No doubt the sprawl was the result of this having been two communities, twin cities that amalgamated, referred to as North Port and South Port, all of which is now Port Alberni.

I made my way to the harbour, the inland end of the inlet, fed from a creek and two lakes. A sign led me to the site of ancient Indigenous petroglyphs, likely left by the ancestors of the area's Hupačasath First Nation, a name meaning "people residing above the water." Although eroded and faint, the symbols in stone are still legible, a collection of waterborne creatures. Some appear mythic, one a cross between wolf and sea lion, another that resembles a tortoise, one more a high-dorsal-finned whale, likely an orca. Plus a snarling sea serpent, as though I'd stumbled onto a saltwater version of Ogopogo, the Spirit of Lake Okanagan.

In the midst of Port Alberni, fronting the long snaking fjord, a smell of pulp hung, the aroma of forestry, perhaps future pages for books. Hillsides bracketing the water were a checkerboard patchwork of clearcut and reforestation, like a haphazard lawn mown over staggering days, or a fairway groomed for its golfers.

The city and surrounding valley were named after Don Pedro de Alberní, Spanish commander of Fort San Miguel at Nootka Sound, northwest of here on the Pacific coast, at the end of a string of provincial parks. All of this being Nuu-chah-nulth land, the proper name for what's known as Nootka. Where I was, in the centre of town, is home to Hupačasath and Tseshaht, part of the Nuu-chah-nulth Nations, Indigenous language still evident in place names such as Somass, Kitsuksis, and Pacheena.

I wandered the multi-use pier and waterfront shops of the quay, where a few retailers had festive displays. A gaggle of pensioners had gathered around a cluster of vintage cars, peering under hoods, toeing tires. Next door, a donut shop sign read, *Best*

Donuts on Vancouver Island. I ate two with red and green sprinkles, and didn't disagree.

Strolling the quay I passed a fountain, water trickling on concrete. A clocktower looked on, exterior stairs painted red, next to chainsaw sculptures of raptors and salmon. Nearby, a carved eagle, open-winged, crowned a totem, the look of a cormorant airing its feathers. The eagle was clutching a salmon, all of this in sawn cedar. Beyond the walkway, water stretched in both directions.

I stopped to read a plaque detailing Canada's Merchant Navy, "The Lifeline of the World," commemorating the World Wars and Korean conflict. Apart from a small motorboat carving its way up the inlet, the water was undisturbed, the space peaceful. Even the grey-haired contingent ogling cars seemed muted, the landscape demanding an almost reverential hush.

I scrutinized this funnel-like valley, geography that touches the sea, part of the Pacific Ring of Fire that's so susceptible to seismic activity. In 1946, an earthquake shook the region – 7.3 on the Richter scale – Canada's largest recorded onshore quake. Apart from its intensity, what made it unusual is that unlike most tremors in the area, which are tectonic in nature, the 1946 quake was a crustal event, a breakdown in the earth's lithosphere, resulting in one of BC's most damaging quakes, with shocks felt up and down the mainland from Alaska to Oregon.

Later, I read of this event as a footnote in a book by Roderick Haig-Brown, when he lived in Elk River, just north of here. He described the quake as it shook nails from siding and walls, his home defying long odds and staying upright, albeit askew.

In 1964, Port Alberni was struck once again, with a quake and subsequent tsunami that flooded the valley. Water rose half a metre in barely a minute, surpassing the high-water mark by two and a half metres. Dozens of homes washed away, yet miraculously, no one was injured.

Being there, I had a distinct sense of being on the cusp of the world. Maybe proximity to the earth's natural forces, echoes of quakes and tsunamis. Or it might've been knowing this watery snake of an inlet joins the Pacific Ocean, which covers a third of the globe. The perspective of magnitude left me feeling particularly inconsequential, but with an awareness of connection to everything. A sensation of significant insignificance.

In the late 1780s, Frances and William Barkley explored this area under the British flag, giving Barkley Sound its name, just beyond my view at the mouth of Alberni Inlet. Frances, it's said, was the first European woman to visit what's now BC, her name given to a ferry that still shuttles passengers through the inlet. She's considered the "first woman to circumnavigate the globe without deception," referring to the fact

European women *did* crew vessels sailing around the world but previously went incognito, forced to disguise themselves as men.

This area also had Hudson's Bay Company ties in the mid-1800s, when Adam Horne mapped an overland route crossing Vancouver Island, utilizing Indigenous trails leading here from the Island's east shore. It was the time of the American Civil War, when the US interstate lumber trade virtually ceased, creating a need for foreign lumber. In response to this burgeoning market, local sawmills were built and the valley became a forestry hub, taking advantage of abundant timber with convenient transport means along rivers and seaboard.

Gold was later discovered, with a few modest rushes in the latter half of the 19th century and into the mid-20th century. When the Canadian Pacific Railway was being constructed, late in the 1800s, surveyor A.B. Rogers came here, plotting a course for the line, and gave Rogers Creek its moniker. This is the same man after whom BC's Rogers Pass is named, the mountainous gap in Glacier National Park. Rogers also mapped Montana's high col crossing the Continental Divide. The name he gave *that* one? Rogers Pass. I can only assume that shortly thereafter Rogers was asked to stop naming things.

"Say, I got a good name for it!"

"Yeah, Rogers, we know. Any *other* suggestions?"

WHERE SPIRITUALITY AND RELIGION MIGHT MEET

With memories of the west set aside for the moment, I'm continuing up the east of the Island, the starboard side of this ocean canoe. I stop at Qualicum Beach to stroll the sand at low tide, with views of Hornby, Denman, Texada, and Lasqueti Islands lying to the north, east, and south. Sunshine breaks through, and apart from the chill it feels just like summer. A few bivalves and gulls on the sand. A heron takes off from the tideline. The sun brightens. I peel off two sweaters and feel like I'm cheating the season.

On the broad stretch of beach a few sand dollars, each belly design reminding me of a snowflake or tree-topping star. Then an *actual* star. An ochre starfish, or sea star, still floppy with life, a neat five-pointed sample. (I've seen others with multiple arms, a kind of regenerative defence, like a mythical hydra.) I could imagine stringing a few of these purply baubles on a Scots pine or spruce for nautical seaside festivities. (But not live ones, of course.)

Now I've picked up a trail into old growth. In the heart of the town, a Heritage Forest, and in the middle of *that* sits a thick slice of timber set upright on its edge, enabling viewers to see, even count, its growth rings. Dendrochronology. This one has a few hundred rings, indicating its age when felled. Beside it, a timeline details what was happening around the globe as the tree lived its life.

1515: This Douglas fir seedling sprouts into sunlight after a forest fire.
1520: Ferdinand Magellan circumnavigates the globe.
1579: Francis Drake explores the British Columbia coast.
1700: A 9.0 earthquake and tsunami hits Vancouver Island.
1774: Juan Pérez explores this coastline.
1776: First smallpox epidemic decimates Coastal First Nations.
1778: Captain Cook comes through.
1792: Captain Vancouver charts the area.
1812: Britain defeats the US for control of Canada.
1820: Sea otters near extinction.
1846: 49th parallel established as Canada–US boundary.

1849: Vancouver Island, now a British Crown colony, is leased to Hudson's Bay Company.
1862: A second smallpox epidemic devastates the Island's Indigenous population.
1871: BC joins the Dominion and Emily Carr is born in Victoria.
1876: The Pentlatch Nation Qualicum Band Reserve is established.
1885: Canadian Pacific Railway completed and BC enters Confederation.
1910: This fir is felled, using a team of horses. It was 400 years old.

Four hundred years in concentric rings, a two-dimensional map pulled from a vertical realm. I consider the stories layered in each ring of growth. Flashbacks to my small disc of alder that accompanied me through those Okanagan seasons as well, melding freshwater and salt.

Turning from the historical wood slab, I pick up the trail where the forest borders a creek. Sword ferns duel in the undergrowth, and I push through salal to approach a monstrous fir, 50 metres high, 800 years old. The giant seems to anchor and enrich the forest, infusing the space with new oxygen. No need to count rings or read plaques; simply stop, be, and breathe. The dates I've just read become meaningless, time turning fluid and endless. It's a place I don't want to leave.

I recall the notion of being in one's "thin place." A term derived from Celtic lore, a thin place is that blur where spirituality and religion might meet, bumping like boats on shared hawsers. It's said that your thin place is that spot where your higher self is revealed, where barriers between here and elsewhere, the past and beyond, are thinner. Whether these barriers are real, imposed, or imagined, I can't say. Likely all of those things. But here, in the trees, with air brushing limbs overhead, it's a truly thin place. Another space where I feel a belonging. Like much of this season, a thin edge to a wedge, finding balance, that overlap of spirit and faith with those tangible things we might touch, taste, and smell.

Off the main path is a side trail, even thinner, where I navigate tree roots and deadfalls. A storm clearly blew through only recently – fresh snaps on boughs, big fallen branches, litters of twigs, fallen cones. Then the cluster of pine opens up, revealing a wide grassy lea, a pupil to the conifer iris. And there in the heart of this forest of green, a slender blue spruce, a virtual match to the one growing outside the *chabad* in Nanaimo.

At a glance the solitary tree almost looks ostracized, other evergreens keeping a distance. But of course, the spruce likely found its own place in the clearing, perhaps where lightning once struck. The more I look at this pillar of needles in festive blue green the more I see it as self-assured, a slight sway all its own, the centre of the dance floor. No doubt hearing its own drumbeat, an arboreal dance or the rhythm, perhaps, of flight.

On through the forest, where I find a scatter of art drops – a small line of ladybug rocks, hand-painted in yuletide red, creeping through Celtic green moss. Next to this, a termite mound climbs between cedars. I've been here before, summer visits over several years, and am aware of this gold-coloured mound, the termite home, slowly growing at the pace of a stalagmite. Something about it reminds me of the methodical garden growth orchestrated by Jennie Butchart, only here it's both flora and fauna, living on moss-covered limestone.

Ahead, I spot a feather on the ground from an owl, shades of tawny, light brown, and cream. A curve of serration on one side indicates raptor, predators that dive onto prey. Which I learned from a birder, who, rather wonderfully, was named Robin.

The forest's aglow in its palette of greens. There's a crosshatch of timber, most of it fallen, some cut, all melting into the undergrowth. Blankets of moss cover stumps and earthen patches while salal gives the space the look of a vase awaiting fresh roses. Evergreen needles and soft cones give way underfoot, while overhead a few rays of sun shine on finger-like boughs.

I've seen a few walkers with dogs, but the woods still feel private. Something about the old growth, a cushion of moss, as though someone's hit mute on an unseen remote. That sensation of air being richer, an infusion of oxygen. Just off the trail a sign catches my eye, "Logging History," by a huge cedar stump with rectangular indentations around its perimeter, next to a black-and-white photo taken a century ago. In the shot, a lumberjack has a plank jammed into one of the notches and is standing, elevated, a metre above the ground, as though perched on a small diving board.

The logger's in the process of working a three-metre-long, two-handled saw. The scale of the task is inconceivable, like cutting a house in half, horizontally. And I think of the time dad and I tackled a gnarly old hawthorn with a saw that looked much like that, though not nearly as long. An exercise in futility. But here in the photo, there's no doubt the tree's coming down. The sign by the picture reads, "Notches in the stump show where loggers stood on springboards to get above the butt swell for easier crosscut sawing by hand." The cedar stump, now ensconced in moss and salal, resembles a gargantuan bundle of raw pasta, a fistful of spaghetti awaiting the drop to hot water. It's actually several trees that grew apart, then together, having disbanded but united again, regrouping to form a community.

1944
POLAR EXPRESS

Previous spread: Polar Express, Ladysmith Festival of Lights

Above: Polar Express, Ladysmith Light Up

POLAR EXPRESS

St. Anne's Anglican Church, built in 1894, Parksville

Eagle and Salmon, carved by Karl Morgan

Overleaf: Seriously Festive Sweater

Mailbox to the North Pole

Hotel Grand Pacific in Gingerbread, Habitat for Humanity Fundraiser

A PLATTER OF DEWY SNOW MIST

Back in the car I pass Milner Gardens, the beauty of Butchart on a compact scale. The facility's not yet open; no lights, scones, or tea. I'll need to return on a weekend. Leaving the seaside, I turn the car slightly to continue up-Island, as though aiming toward the North Pole.

By Little Qualicum River a bald eagle tops a monstrous dead tree, a living ornament in cocoa-white feathers, grander than my envisioned tree-topping sea star. Up ahead, a fresh string of *C*s: Courtenay, Comox, Campbell River. Along Whiskey Creek, more trees in red and green tones. Farther north, the radio muddles a mixture of static and stations. Country music now clear, a new carol with slide guitar, and the vintage lyrical pairing of *winter snow* and *mistletoe*.

Road signs warn of elk, icy bridges, and slippery roads, conditions not unlike a North Island wedding we attended in Telegraph Cove. It was a lovely summer affair, guests from all over. Three big elk and then a black bear came through. Out-of-towners were impressed, recalling old jokes of lacing up sneakers when seeing a bear.

"You can't outrun a bear," someone says to the sneaker-lacer.

To which the sneaker-lacer replies, "I don't need to outrun the bear, I just need to outrun *you*."

Which likely explained the impeccably dressed bride and groom wearing sneakers. (They weren't *really* wearing sneakers, but it's more fun to imagine they were.)

I keep driving and the ground opens up around Big Qualicum River, a bowl stretching from mountains to sea. A jet overhead is heading north, its jet stream a mirror of my vehicle exhaust in the cold.

A bridge crosses Thames Creek, a reminder of settlers. On the radio, ads for gingerbread houses and fundraisers with cocoa for kids. Another encourages shoppers to come by the local tree lot, almost a plea, as their Christmas supply isn't being depleted. Good prices, they say, a selection of pines. And I wonder if it's too early, or if money is collectively tight, or perhaps there's a trend away from live trees.

By the road I spot a perfectly symmetrical lodgepole pine growing wild that looks inverted, its branches resembling a menorah. A juvenile eagle flaps by, an expanse of wings like a plane. More snow in the hills, now gleaming in sun. Past Buckley Bay, with ferries to Denman and Hornby Islands.

On to Union Bay and through Royston. Two ravens in flight at head-height frame the road, moving landmarks the colour of onyx.

Now into the Comox Valley, on Ginger Goodwin Way. Redhead Albert Goodwin, nicknamed Ginger, was a coal miner here, one of the first advocates for workers' rights and unionization in British Columbia. Low wages and poor working conditions were what Goodwin fought, leading strikes and taking part in the development of the BC Federation of Labour. Also an opponent of military conscription, Goodwin came under increased scrutiny during the First World War. In 1918 he was killed by law enforcement, the case around it still vague. A general strike followed in Vancouver, an outpouring of support and anger around Goodwin's death, also considered a catalyst for the 1919 Winnipeg general strike.

Here on the road, the sky overhead is impossibly blue as I keep heading north. Signs for Mount Washington, ferries, an airport, and an exit lead me to Courtenay. A road sign shows a tractor: *Farm route*. Next to this, a yellow diamond: *Bike route*. On the outskirts of Courtenay and Comox I catch a faint whiff of woodfire, then see murals on walls along traffic-calmed streets.

Trees here strike me as larger. Maybe the lay of the land, maybe perspective – a craning effect. I park and walk through Courtenay downtown. Stop for lunch:

soup, sandwich, and spicy hot chai. Outside, two ravens shoulder past overhead, with crows in abundance, but no sign of the vultures that gyre in clumps through the rest of the year. Maybe they follow the snowbirds elsewhere (the birds *and* the people).

A stroll to Sid Williams Theatre in sharp-angled sun, forced to squint from under my toque. Ribboned wreaths adorn lampposts, the look of a ring toss and feel of a fairground. Historic pictures decorate the exterior of the Courtenay and District Museum and Palaeontology Centre. I pop in and delve back in time through displays of Indigenous art, old rocks, and bone. A sign advertises world-famous fossil tours.

A woman named Laura is at the front desk, and I ask how she likes the season.

"It's quiet." She laughs. "Which is just fine by me."

The exhibits are excellent, a small space with rich content. Prehistoric and Indigenous. An elasmosaur skeleton wears a festive-trimmed hat next to carved Salish masks: a raven and bear, decorated with actual feathers and hair in ebony and ruby red paint. More history, artwork, and skeletons. Then Laura gives me a wave as I take my leave, and head to another yuletide performance.

Under poles with garland and wreaths the theatre has a long line of ticketholders, all wearing red, folks dressed for the season and show. Inside, the decor is full festive. Massive pine boughs with wreaths on the walls, trees on the stage, lights overhead, a healthy dose of red, gold, and glitter. "Jingle Bell Rock" pumps from the sound system. Flashbacks to high school gym, our wintertime class in phys ed, three weeks of dance, line dancing to this song. Another musical loop I can't shake, but don't really mind. I got a B, by the way, improving my grade-point average.

The show here is *The Yellowpoint Spectacular*, part Broadway, part Cotton Club, part burlesque, with enough yuletide to fit with the season. Talented musicians, dancers, and singers. An enthusiastic full house. I admit I was expecting more Frosty and Rudolph. To my surprise a sombre performance mid-show, a tribute to Jesus. Then to my even greater surprise, it segues into the Rolling Stones' "Sympathy for the Devil." In a way, all-inclusive.

Between songs, a few stories, some trivia, audience contests with prizes.

"In the movie *Christmas Vacation*, what kind of mugs are Eddie and Clark using for eggnog?"

"Who starred in *The Santa Clause*?"

"What's 'Merry Christmas' in Spanish?"

Winners are chosen, prizes awarded.

The show's been touring through the festive season for years, this time hitting three Island venues: where I am now, Sid Williams Theatre in Courtenay, as well as the Port Theatre in Nanaimo, and McPherson Playhouse in Victoria's Centennial Square, scene of the festive white lights with totems and trees.

The show concludes and I drive away under gossamer sky, sun setting in blue. A stream of crows fly west as I steer toward the water to follow the coast and head south. A festively dressed tractor sits by the road, and the Trent River is high, now topping its banks. Onward to Fanny Bay, growing oysters in farms. Past aging ships, an array of decay at a boatyard surrounded in trees.

At Union Bay, a clearcut field awaits development, and a tall inukshuk sits on a heavy breakwater, a rock finger pointing seaward. The ocean today is as calm as the pond with the cattle I passed farther south. By the ferry to Denman Island, a motionless heron hunts in the shallows, while a gull drops mussels on rocks. There's a brief waft of skunk from somewhere. Now, for the afternoon drive, the on-air radio personality asks callers, "Let us know what you think of the company trend to move Christmas parties to January."

Lighthouse Gift Shop has a roadside display of flat, painted trees, lined up like signs. Red, green, and white, in two dimensions, the look of a tree lot in Asian scroll art. Across the water, Texada Island is topped with a meringue puff of cloud, a clown wig in white. The next story bleats from the radio: "Things people have found in their Christmas trees, *after* they've gotten them home." The story continues. "In Texas, a live possum that emerged a week later. In California, a hatch of praying mantises that burst from the branches." I change the station, happy to have a fake tree.

Past Qualicum First Nation, there's a fork in the road: *19, 19A*. I choose the latter and carry on along the Oceanside Route, where a pocket of smoke eases through trees, the smell seeping through closed windows. I bypass turnoffs to Spider and Horne Lakes, memories of caving and summertime hikes. A sign by a campsite: *Closed for the season.* A dragon boat sits on a lawn, its prow the head of a raven in Salish design. Which gets me thinking again about the Island from above, this ocean vessel of forest and stone. Perhaps more accurate than I'd imagined, as according to geological surveys, the land is in fact inching seaward, slowly moving away from the mainland.

Most of the interpretive and artistic displays I've enjoyed through this excursion, I now realize, are those I consider most stylized, like that boat on the lawn with its raven design. A reimagining of places and perspectives. Ancient traditions along with the new on this Island canoe, geography as a cornucopia horn, spilling with heritage, wildlife, and forest. Each facet a celebration of people and place.

Over the water, sunset is a pink and peach blaze. To the east, snow-dusted mountains stand guard on the mainland. From the highway a side road cuts to the shore through monstrous firs, two centuries old. A trawler carves through the bay, muscling into waves. I spot roosts where eagles hunt, scouting the surf and the tideline. By a forest, a few single trees are wearing bright lights as though dressed for a party, encouraging their friends to join in. Across Parksville and Qualicum's town-to-town trail, sasquatch footprints in yellow traipse north. Maybe left by the Cameron Lake nudist. Then again, at this time of year, the prints might belong to a yeti.

A rabbit hops down railway tracks, flashes of cottony white on the ties. A cherry tree looms, ponderous, a trigger of seasonal memories. Under setting sun sky, an inversion of fog is reflecting the tangerine sunset. Past Englishman River Falls, more recollection of excursions and discovery, at the moment served on a platter of dewy snow mist. ❖

THIN PLACES AND A PILOT NAMED CHRISTMAS

I take a break from the road, but not the season. Find a café in Courtenay, settle in with croissant and coffee, and scroll through photos, recalling a few festive memories. One being the time Deb and I left on a flight on December 24th, crossing the dateline, east to west, skipping the 25th altogether. I dozed off on Christmas Eve and woke up on Boxing Day. What might be a child's nightmare was a novelty as a grown-up. The pilot's name on that flight? Dave Christmas.

"You're kidding?!" I said to the flight attendant, who laughed.

"Uh, *no*," he smiled. "Always fun, but right now, extra special."

On the wall, here in the café, a few musical instruments have been hung as décor. A guitar with a broken G-string, which makes me smile. Next to that, a blue ukelele, reminding me of perhaps the best present ever: a song, "Aloha 'Oe," given to me in Hawaii. A song of separation, yet connection, the tune was written by Princess Lili'uokalani, the young woman lyrically gifting her partner some flowers. The song knows no season, but it became a carol when a woman we called Auntie Tutu shared it with me at this time of year in the form of sheet music. A yuletide memento. Then we played that same song in a ukelele ensemble under palms wrapped in lights, all of us wearing holiday flair – bright floral shirts, muumuus, seashells, and leis.

On another occasion we celebrated the season near the birthplace of Sinterklaas, the lowlands of western Europe. On a table a whirligig turned, carved in blond wood with lit candles beneath, Saint Nick spinning with presents and kids. The angle of whirligig blades had to be set just right; an angle too sharp or obtuse and Nick would dance in reverse, doing a festive moonwalk, a fun but off-putting visual. On Christmas Eve, we stayed up with children to follow the NORAD Santa-tracker as it circled the globe. In the morning, I walked to a bakery to pick up a yule log, not for the fire but dessert, covered in icing and fruit. Walking home, I cut through a forest, towering trees with bare branches laced high overhead, limbs linked in a version of "here is the church and here is the steeple." A creek burbled, a quiet and ancient locale, terrain where Odin led yuletide hunts, with the same feel as that Grimm

Brothers grove in Nanaimo. If it were dark I'd have likely been scared, but on that day, in the muting of fog, it was a place of intimate spirituality.

Another unique memory was a December spent in the heat of a southern hemisphere summer, hearing the same songs we hear in the north, carols playing in stores. "Oh, the weather outside is frightful!" At the time it was sunny, cloudless, and blistering hot. I then learned that particular song, composed by Jule Styne and Sammy Cahn, was written in a California heat wave, 1945. Someone in the Hollywood studio had said, somewhat wistfully, "Let it snow! Let it snow! Let it snow!" Or at least that's the story.

Finished with coffee and nostalgia for the moment, I stroll a mid-Island street and savour window displays, pine boughs with ornaments, light strands, and holly. A mail carrier is wearing an elf hat. A postbox is painted in gold, labelled *Letters to Santa*. I pop into a shop, strike up conversation with Frances, and ask her about this time of year.

"Well, I'm from the Philippines," she says, "and the festive season's *very* important to us. *All* the families get together. We start celebrating in September, then carry on all through the 'ber months."

"The *brrr* months?" I ask, uncertain.

She chuckles. "The *'ber* months. You know, September, October, November, December. All the way through until Christmas." She smiles, nods. "It's *big*."

Making me realize I, too, could experience this season for much of the year, and with renewed festive vigour I fight the urge to add eggnog to everything: cereal, oatmeal, coffee. And instead nibble cinnamon-infused chocolate, wondering if my choice is any healthier. So I eat a Mandarin orange. Which makes me laugh, remembering dad, orange missiles, and misunderstandings. I scan the guide on TV. Upcoming movies: *Home Alone*, *Die Hard*, *Elf*, *A Christmas Story*. More carols on loop, decorations in silver and blue. I feel a pattern recurring, so to shed some fresh light – light that's *not* red and green – I reach out to my friend Reverend Stephen, a retired minister I first met at a poetry reading.

Without lead-in, I ask him, "Tell me what the season means to you."

His reply is immediate. "It's a festive time," he says, "for my wife Jenny and me. One of spiritual as well as practical preparation. We keep Advent as just that, preparation, saving Christmas for the 12 days of the festival, beginning December 25th."

Which has me recalling Ukrainian friends: 12 dishes, 12 days, an Orthodox past aligning with present-day customs.

Stephen expands on his favoured traditions. "We celebrate the feast of the incarnation, knowing the presence of God in our hearts. The festive season is this miracle. Family, friends, the familiar, traditional, treasured memories – these are the context of transcendent experience."

And I think once again of that thin place, thin *places*, where we feel immediately present, on-task and belonging – whether bathing in a forest, meditating, or praying in a temple, a synagogue, a mosque, or a church. No doubt every song that I heard in stage plays, and in the Cathedral, was a thin place for those in attendance: singing, lighting candles, sharing transcendent experience.

Being a natural orator, Stephen concludes with an allegorical story, a true tale I believe, with substance. I feel as though I'm holding a finger on ribbon as he continues, cinching a bow on his gift.

"Some years ago, a reporter asked four international ambassadors what their wishes would be for the season.

"'Peace on earth,' said the first.

"'Cooperation between nations,' said the second.

"'Fair sharing of resources,' said the third.

"Then the last person said, almost sheepishly, 'Well, I'm actually hoping for a box of candy.'"

To which Stephen rounds off his story. "And whose wish was most likely fulfilled?" A pause, as the imagined giftwrap is removed.

"The moral, to be thankful that we don't always get what we deserve, and we do sometimes get what we don't deserve."

All I can do is thank Stephen. The story, perfectly open-ended to a degree. Objective. Shared perspective, two sides of an insightful coin. Perhaps even one made of candy. ❖

MAYBE A WHOLE WORLD UP THERE

Again I'm mid-Island, near Qualicum, surrounded in festive displays. And I swing by Nourish Farm, a place Deb and I have stayed previously. On the property, a barn trimmed in red is next to green gardens, all of it nestled in forest. The land had been logged, a few gnarled fists of pine knuckles evidence of this, until Cindy and Lorne bought the property, both leaving long-term careers to come here and learn how to farm: clear the land, build a home, plant a garden.

Now the garden and farm are established. Bees have moved in to cross-pollinate, fitting a piece into a much bigger puzzle. From our second-floor room we looked over berries and herbs in tidy neat rows with a palette of seasonal vegetables. The bees hummed between flowers, holding the jigsaw together, not only surviving but thriving. Chickens were scratching about, very much free range, meandering through trees in the forest. Cindy explained she often had to search the woods for freshly laid eggs; a real-life, year-round Easter egg hunt.

One morning, while there, we woke to a pallor of sun, the low wattage of hospital rooms. It felt like a day to be indoors so I went to the Qualicum Beach Museum, where a carved totem fronted the building with a patch of manicured flowers. Across the road sat the former railway station, part of the E&N line, dowdy yet proud, painted the red of a holiday cardigan. A church was next door to that, with its own compact round garden. From above it must look like a colourful crop-circle.

The museum exterior was rugged red brick, inside were displays of a logging and railway past. A century ago a hotel sat here, a few of its furnishings still on display. Next to this, a paleontology exhibit featuring Rosie the Walrus. Rosie being the fossilized skeleton of an adult female walrus who lived here 60,000 years ago. Found in clay down the hill by the sand where I saw the sea star, Rosie is the best-preserved Pleistocene walrus specimen in western North America.

The story of Rosie's discovery is a good one. One of teamwork. In 1979, a local resident was walking this beach, gathering oysters for lunch, when he saw what he thought was a jaw bone protruding from sand. Prying it free he took the bone home, then his daughter took it to school, where her teacher identified it as a fossil. The three then returned to the beach at low tide; more bones were discovered, and before long the complete skeleton of the prehistoric walrus was revealed.

What adds to the story is that as news of the discovery grew, so too did the team of volunteers, helpers, and experts. Another local – a visually impaired man – located the smallest bones, which were only discernible by touch. Through the scatter of rocks, he *felt* his way along the shoreline, sourcing the delicate metacarpal and phalange bones of the walrus's finger-like flippers. Fully reassembled, Rosie was here for a decade before being moved to the Canadian Museum of Nature in Ottawa. What's still here, under glass, is a cast recreation of Rosie's skull with her tusks, displayed next to one of her ribs.

This played in my mind, beachcombing and unearthing time, when I returned to the water with a kayak. Tide was high and mercifully I didn't have to lug the boat far. Tossing my shoes in the craft, I eased into the seat, gripped the paddle, and thrust myself into the surf. On the surface a shoal of fingerlings swirled, tiny dorsals in silvered pirouettes. A seal approached, accompanied me for a while, then disappeared with a nostrilly breath and a glint of dark blubber.

Paddling the curve of the bay, I aimed for the next pointed headland. Two bald eagles sat shoulder to shoulder in a towering fir, the top of the tree bare and dead. Their roost had the look of a mariner's crow's nest, mixing the avian metaphor. From another perch, a juvenile eagle took flight, maybe the offspring of the pair in the mast-like pine. The brown-headed juvie flew directly over, its flightpath dead straight and level, 20 metres above the water. As I swivelled to watch, it dropped like a deadweight, struck the surface with the subtlest splash, and rose with a wet flopping fish in its talons. The fish looked to be maybe two kilos, a decent meal. But as the eagle flew back toward shore something wasn't quite right. The bird fussed, as though unsure if it wanted to grasp its meal in talons or beak. An awkward bit of flying ensued, the raptor almost folding in two (like when dad caught the orange with his tentacles). Then the bird dropped the fish, a wriggling, plummeting gleam striking the sea with a *sploosh*, where it swam away into deepening malachite shades. The eagle, however, didn't change course, just returned to its perch a short distance away.

What had I witnessed? Was that a mistake? Was the young eagle learning to hunt, the way an infant might struggle to hold a spoon? Or did the bird decide the fish was a throw-back? A raptor's version of catch-and-release. The more I thought about it, the more I thought of the fish and the tale it could share with its schoolmates.

"I tell ya, there's a *whole world* up there!"

"Sure," one of the others would say, with an eye roll. "And you *flew*. With an *eagle*, no less."

A reminder, perhaps, not to discount what others might share, and what they know to be true.

THICK OF THE SEASON

Farther north, still on the east of the Island, the weather holds. I follow the pebbly shore where the Northern Gulf Islands dot the horizon, beaches that offer up fossils to prospectors with patience or skill. Maybe another sample like Rosie, but most often ammonites, found in abundance around here, usually in rocks the size of bowling balls, along with fossilized seaweed and leaves. Former ocean bed reveals itself, slowly climbing, maybe one day to form a new mountain.

I've made my way to Campbell River, a town of forestry, fishing, and residual mining. Energy as well, with hydroelectric generators on rivers and falls. Strolling through town, I admire carved art, stories of commerce and lineage. Chainsaw sculptures in cedar: mariners, lumberjacks, anglers. Wildlife carvings as well: eagles and ravens, salmon and orcas, black bears and wolves. Each stump's gently weathered, colours having shifted from the freshly-cut shades of coral and honey to dried silver and soft granite grey. Many of the pieces are now wearing festive red hats and lights.

The town extends in a long slender neck, much like the spit fronting Comox. Everything, it seems, is a short stroll from the sea. An eagle flies by, while a flock of black-and-white Bonaparte's gulls shriek as they bob in the shallows, resembling small skuas or terns. The ruckus is deafening but nothing to do with the eagle, just a raft of cacophonous birds.

Continuing my drive, I'm now in the thick of the season. There's a truck with a red Rudolph nose on its grille. A car has faux antlers protruding from windows. A tour bus is strung with bright flashing lights. And a sedan has stripey elf legs dangling from its trunk, the small passenger, presumably, squashed next to a jack and spare tire. On the radio, an announcement for the Frank Ney Memorial Polar Bear Swim, taking place in Nanaimo. I shiver just thinking of that, even more than when watching those late-season swimmers near Shirley.

A slight turn inland, the coast fading behind me. Winding highway leads to dense forest, where I park and pick up a trail for a few kilometres, out and back, with enough undulation to have me huffing up hills. Cedars and firs and peekaboo views. At one end of the trail a waterfall rumbles through narrows as the path carries on by a river, its surface the look of a lake. Here, power generators grasp the tumble and flow of freshwater.

A sign warns of a bear, but the caution doesn't look new, no dates on the sign. I assume the risk is low. Maybe they're in hibernation by now. Another sign warns of a cougar, but this one is dated, a sighting last week. A grasshopper leaps from the scrub. (Don't *they* hibernate?) This trail is a space of wildflowers through much of the year. Now it's just stocks and stems with spindly trees, a litter of leaves on the ground.

To one side of the trail is a huge and lone spruce, growing and healthy, but with a natural hollow in the trunk, as though fitted with a shadowy door. The opening enters the base of the tree like a portal, leaving me to wonder who might be inside. It reminds me of a southern hemisphere kauri museum, where a trunk like this is displayed, only much, much bigger. A logger had further hollowed it out with an axe and a saw, carving the interior of the massive old stump into a home for his family. A multi-level, multi-room house for five people, with an interior spiralling stairwell joining each room, all carved from the single piece of wood. No planking. No glueing or nails. One. Solid. Piece. The most ingenious artisanal creation I've seen. How do you envision that? Working in reverse to create ceilings and floors, stairwells and walls within a single block of timber? A home in a holiday tree. (And no, the occupants weren't elves. They were Kiwis. Not the fruit or the birds, but the likeable people who mispronounce "fish and chips.")

Now, leaving the forested park, I have a choice to make. Stay on the east side of the Island, or follow the highway S-curves pointing west, paralleling a river to the ocean. The owner of the place I rented in Campbell River, a restorer of vintage motorbikes, lovingly spoke of this roadway. Quiet, curvaceous, smooth asphalt, a road built for riding. But not for me now. Not at this time of the year.

Gold River, the town down the road, reminds me of Port Alberni, another inland community that's part of the coast, claw marks of sea and long craggy fjords. Only here, in the geographical centre of the Island, a narrow band of freshwater connects to an inlet before joining the North Pacific. There's a ferry connecting this westerly coast, joining oceanfront outposts. One of these outposts is called Friendly Cove, the place Captain Cook first set foot in this part of the world, here on Nuu-chah-nulth land. Once home to 20 longhouses and 1500 residents, the settlement now has six inhabitants, with two lighthouse keepers. The very thought of which makes me lonely.

At the fork in the road, I stick with my plan to stay east, and venture back to Campbell River's historically rich, geographically small peninsula, to Tyee Spit, at the mouth of the river with the same name as the town. The sea today is indigo with a northerly wind frothing the surface. I find some informative plaques and learn some more history.

A black and white aerial photo of where I'm standing shows the estuary jammed with logs. A descriptor accompanying the image explains that local forestry began in the 1880s, with a camp on the Quinsam River, which feeds into the Campbell River just west of here. The confluence is known as Nunn's Creek, and felled timber lashed into long floating log booms filled this space well into the 1990s. In 1912, renowned angler Sir John Rogers was quoted as saying it was "now practically useless from the fishermen's point of view, the river for about a mile from its mouth is practically blocked with great rafts of enormous logs." Ironically, or tragically, this was one of the world's most abundant areas for wild salmon: chinook, sockeye, chum, coho, and pink.

The next photo, this one from the 1970s, shows a long, slender pier in the lee of the spit, the wharf lined with floatplanes. From what was touted as the busiest seaplane base in the world, these single-engine craft hauled supplies and equipment, served as medivac transport, and shuttled workers to hundreds of logging camps. But from the 1980s onward, industry eliminated smaller operations. Consolidation combined with improved roads, ferries, high speed crew-boats, and helicopters reduced floatplane use, although they remain a vital link for many islanders.

Another photo grabs my attention, this one unlike the rest. Taken up close, the subjects are rigidly posed. Two men stand between tents, rough canvas on poles. A boy sits on the ground beside them, perhaps one of their sons. A rack's been constructed, two spars with a crosspiece, and from the beam hang two 50-pound salmon (20-plus kilos). Each fish is larger than the boy in the picture. There's a dog standing on a bundle that's perched on a barrel and box, the canine the tallest one in the photo. A second black dog lies next to the boy on the ground. Both dogs, the boy, and one man look directly into the camera, the men and the boy with stern expressions – the look of everyone in vintage photos. Both dogs, however, sport big happy smiles.

A final photo sits near the end of a short looping path. It's a shot of the wood framed Quartell Big House that once stood here. The proper name of the former building is written on a placard as *Kweladzatse*, the structure owned by Wei Wai Kum First Nation of the Laich-Kwil-Tach, part of the Kwakwa̱ka̱'wakw Nations. The picture was taken in 1923, the last remaining big house on Tyee Spit. It was here, in 1914, that representatives of a royal commission first met with locals to discuss land title issues. Issues that remain unresolved. ❁

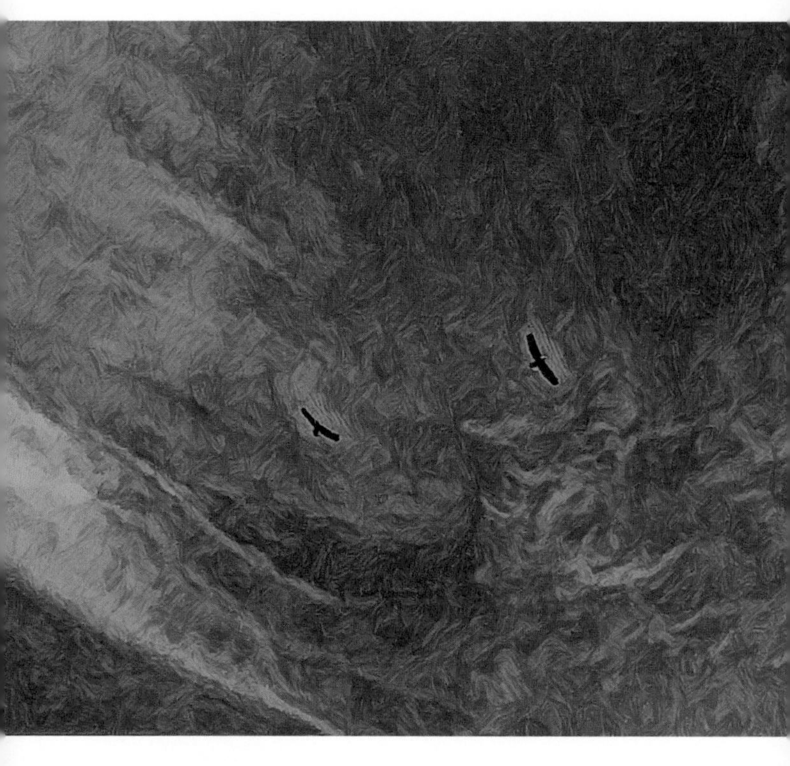

Bald Eagles, Adult and Offspring, near Courtenay

Barred Owl Feather on Nurse Log, Mid Island

Bridge over Little Qualicum River

Ladybug Art Drop, North Island

Fir Trees, Qualicum Beach Heritage Forest

Half Moon, South Island

Overleaf: Inukshuk at Englishman River

TRADITIONS OF GIVING AND SHARING

Taking a break from exploring, I visit with my good friend and writing partner, Mala, whose family heritage has roots in South Asia, Africa, and the South American country of Guyana. One of our recent visits was here on the Island, where we strolled a beach beside Qualicum, watching crustaceans skitter through seagrass ahead of the tide.

"What's festive season mean to you?" I ask.

"Honestly?" she says. "Celebration. And lights."

"What else?"

"Well, when you look around the globe, you see more collectivist cultures. Where celebration means gathering, getting together. But here in North America, or at least north of Mexico, it's more individualistic. The giving of something to someone, and receiving. Again, an exchange between individuals. Which is different from elsewhere."

I nod, understanding, as I hadn't before seen the gift-giving custom with such clarity. Fresh insight from well-travelled friends.

Mala returns to her work, and I'm back in the vehicle, making one more festive pass, a lopsided loop around the mid Island. From the east shore outside Parksville, I drive inland to the village of Coombs, a community bordered by a curved, narrow highway. It's now bright overcast, the sky a dusty chalk smear, and I hope this area will be less busy than it is in the peak summer season. On a pond I see swans, black ones and white, and signs indicating this is home to a bluegrass festival and seasonal rodeo, with a Butterfly World and tropical indoor rainforest. In addition to these, the town's known for its Old Country Market, a place where goats live on the roof.

The quirky feature is now a tourist draw. A thick roof of sod with high wooden walkways allows the goats easy access, where they live a lofty existence for most of the year. Every goat has a name, and you can learn each one's backstory. I see Nibbles, Pip, and Minyon. And happen to know Minyon loves maple leaves and belly rubs, and, no doubt, long walks on the beach at sunset. A few people are taking photos and buying goat paraphernalia. An ever-popular fridge magnet resembles a road sign that warns to watch for goat droppings from above.

The market is a sprawling indoor space with everything you might need for grocery supplies, kitschy household items, and giftware. The market was built by Norwegian settlers Solveig and Kristian Graaten. In their hometown of Lillehammer, sod roof design was common, homes nestled in hillsides, the combination of earth and turf being natural insulators. The fact it's a happy space for goats, it seems, is a bonus.

History here is also unique in that the town was established by the Salvation Army, with immigration encouraged from populous cities in Britain. This took place early in the 20th century. The head of Canada's Salvation Army at the time was Thomas Coombs, for whom this community is named.

My memories of the Salvation Army tend to be fundraisers this time of year: donations on street corners, jangling bells, and felty red hats. For a number of years I cooked in a kitchen at one of the "Sally Ann" community centres, the red emblem creating its own festive feel. The program was one of chef-mentoring and food recovery. Mentees were individuals who weren't easily employable in commercial kitchens, having mental or physical challenges and requiring extra guidance or help. Each individual was remarkably capable, given an environment of patience and tutelage. *Not* the kind of environment you tend to see on celebrity cooking TV.

Food recovery, by the way, was how our kitchen received its ingredients. Food donated by grocery stores that was not yet expired, but retail promotes rapid inventory turn and removal well ahead of best-before dates. Most grocers pay to have this stock removed and disposed of, one of the most wasteful elements in the food industry. However, with a five-ton truck, we gathered good food, brought it back to our kitchen, and prepared healthy meals to freeze and sell at below-market pricing, thereby funding the community centre while offering subsidized meals to anyone in the neighbourhood. The program was exceptional, and I was privileged to be part of it. In its way celebratory and festive but year-round, in the tradition of giving and sharing. ❁

CLOSURE IN A WHISPER OF BREEZE

Again in the car, and it's cold, the sun rising in a stubborn low arc. I've zigzagged eastward and north outside Coombs, now hugging the coast on the Oceanside Route. Past a pub, a gas station, homes facing the sea, a resort amid trees. A turn to the west, the land rising inland, and I enter the community of Cumberland. Approaching town centre, I pass a landscaping business and a yard full of masonry work, then a cenotaph park with a triangle of grass, pruned shrubs and short trees. A village park, water park, Legion, and War Memorial. Cumberland's compact hub has the look of a frontier outpost, with bright buildings in clapboard and a bank built of brick. There's a museum and archives, where I learn a little more history.

This is Coast Salish land, home to the K'omoks, Qualicum, Sliammon (Tla'amin), and Cape Mudge (We Wai Kai) First Nations, along with the Puntledge, or Pentlatch, and Eucletaw (Lekwiltok), also from Cape Mudge, a southern extension of the Kwakwaka'wakw People.

An increasing number of settlers arrived through the mid-19th century, further layering this complex mosaic. For a while, Cumberland boasted Canada's largest Chinatown, and its Japanese community was the largest on the Island. I consider that transition, global growth in a compact expanse, trade routes and transport that followed the original trails through the forest, linking these mountains and shores.

I park the car near the centre of town, where posters advertise more concerts, choirs, and plays taking place in nearby communities. A *Christmas Blues Show* is at Knox United Church in Parksville. *A Fa-La-La Christmas* has what looks like Saint Nick belting out karaoke. Jona & The Yule Lads are performing in Nanaimo. Plus a festive brass performance called *Reindeer Games*. More ads have already been covered over, the signboard thick with upcoming shows and performances already done.

Leaving Cumberland behind, I take the Inland Island Highway – Highway 19 – and turn the car south. In a little under an hour, I'm just outside Qualicum, where I leave the car at the side of the road and head into the woods by Little Qualicum River Fish Hatchery. Here I find a forested footpath of mud, dirt, and pebbles to follow a creek that looks like it might one day grow into a river. A stone's throw away, shelves of water mimic the stream in a series of shallow stepped ladders or locks, from which salmonid species are hatched. Wide-eyed fingerlings make their darting and wriggly way through the murk to the fast-running river and sea. The result? Hopefully, sustainable fish stocks, resulting in a thriving ecological micro-environment. As fish aid the water and tree roots, nitrogen transmuting to oxygenation, other wildlife comes through, nibbling this and that, making babies and what not, and the whole thing, in theory, carries on a bit better than it was prior to us hominids mucking about with it. At least that's the intention. No more ill-conceived introductions, no added shrimp. Just an attempt to assist what ought to be here. All I can say is it makes for a glorious walk.

Birdsong stutters from an overhang of cedar, morse-code music, dashes and dots in the air. A stretch of red foliage peers over the soil, leaning, inching toward a precipice, back to its forest and kin. A spatter of rain releases an aroma of mushrooms and old leaves, the opposite of festive fresh pines.

Through low cloud the sun's almost set, trees cool in peacock and teal, tones of early Picasso. Towering spruce disappear in the light, every one seemingly blue. Ahead, the trail splays into forks, more branches and metaphors. I go left, and then right, breaking from foliage into a meadowy clearing calf-high in grass. A bit farther on, a bat box stands on a pole with no flag, a nation unnamed. At the back of the glade, a triad of spruce stands as one, these ones *actually* blue. Backing onto hemlock and cedar, tall and distinguished, the taller trees have absorbed all the light from the south, leaving the blue trio as facades. Each of the three bursts with life on one side, bushels of blue, their back halves long dead, the look of discarded holiday firs, bare and forlorn. I think of people I've known, myself included, who carry on in this manner, one part facing out, full of life, while the interior shies from the light, from the rest of the world.

A thin whistle wavers from an open-necked bottle between the spruce and a neighbouring cedar, blowing a hollow ghost whisper. Across much of the globe this is the converse of spectres. Spirits are believed to reside in discordant gusts, wind that moans as it passes the lips, the mouth of glass vessels. Some people attach bottles to trees to attract or entrap wraiths in transit. Spiritual wasp traps. Crepe myrtle trees are deemed most effective, and apparently bottles of blue glass work best. This belief comes from an understanding that spirits or pneuma often are caught between worlds, energy swirling in place until resolution permits further progress. In other words, the faltering skirl of a gust, a soft whistle on glass, could mean a loved one is now moving on. A version, perhaps, of that line from *It's a Wonderful Life*, "Every time a bell rings, an angel gets his wings," or something close to it. Closure in a whisper of breeze. ❖

EXTENDED FAMILY

I circle back to the mouth of the Puntledge River in Comox, where much of the community seems to cling to the estuary. Sand and rock join in a long slender neck that stretches into the strait, the peninsula fittingly named Goose Spit. Another link to those vertical stories at Centennial Park in Victoria, specifically, the figure of Beaver. For it was here the Hudson's Bay Company's SS *Beaver* chugged through in the 1830s, looking for trading locales. This site was chosen, the outpost called Komoux, a transliteration of the Indigenous place name, more accurately spelled K'ómoks. Settlers quickly learned of the area's richness and bounty. One British Naval officer noted in 1861 that he'd walked for nearly two days across fertile and arable land, earth he described as being perfectly fit for the plow. This is the same nutrient-rich groundcover that compacted itself into coal, the fuel that powered those later vessels to here. Not quite the coal-lumps in stockings for ill-behaved offspring in lieu of presents this time of year, but I can't help but see a connection.

Now I'm traipsing the shore on an outcrop of basalt and granite. Somewhere beyond, to the east, is the rest of BC, and to the north, Alaska. Behind me, a timber breakwater looks like a fortress. The sun's determined to shine, peeping through fast-moving cloud, but a breeze off the bay keeps the chill of the season on shore.

Following my beach walk I head north, where an extension of forested valley cuts through the Island's interior. This too is K'ómoks land, home to Sahtloot, Sasitla, Ieeksun, and Puntledge Nations. The name of the people and place translates to *plentiful*, indicating this well-soiled land with its profusion of available food, including bear, elk, and deer, salmon and seals, shellfish, herring and cod, ducks and geese, with mushrooms and berries found among forests and undergrowth.

When Francis Drake circled the globe, he came here, in 1579, spending a season restocking his ship with this bounty and trading with locals. He called the area Nova Albion (New Britain), a label he gave much of North America's Pacific coast, an attempt to rebrand terrain that some considered Spanish territory. Although he kept detailed logs, many of Drake's records were lost to fire, leaving precise locations unknown. But most historians agree that Drake and his crew were right here. Spanish explorers Galiano and Flores arrived two centuries later, charting the

Salish Sea, while George Vancouver drew his own detailed maps of this coast in 1792. It was, in a manner, redrawing what already existed in story and song, a translation to flattened dimensions.

Once again I consider my map-art by Nicola North, a reimagining of the land and its coverings. Pulling my print from a slim paper sheath, I realize this is a voice I want to hear, particularly at this time of year, the perspective beyond these colourful brushstrokes.

With a few back and forths we eventually connect, and I thank Nicola for her contribution to the Island community. Then I ask for her thoughts, how she feels about the season.

She thinks before she replies, and I imagine her choosing her hues, the texture and size of paintbrushes. Then she says, "I feel festive when I decorate the tree, which we'll painstakingly choose on a family trip to a tree farm. We have such a meaningful and eclectic collection of ornaments that've been gathered over the past two decades. I cherish the decorations our kids made, and I'm quickly reminded of them running out of school, tenderly holding pipe cleaner snowflakes!"

I love the sensory visual, and encourage her to go on.

"As an artist over the festive period, I take time to slow down, reflect on the year, daydream, and allow the quiet time to let new ideas come to the forefront."

Which I see in the artwork, not only the familiar piece I'm now holding but in her new paintings as well: inspirational, multi-sensory, and regionally proud. Another wave of gratitude, and a sense that I've found yet another relation in this extended and collaborative family. ✿

CONNECTION AND A GIFT UNEXPECTED

I've returned to the southern tip of the Island, as though dotting the base of this seasonal exclamation. I have a short-term rental near Beacon Hill Park in the Victoria neighbourhood of Fairfield. The weather is a bluster, westerlies strafing the sea into whitecaps and 15-knot rollers. Wrapped in an extra two layers, I march toward sunrise, this morning a festive deep red, where melon-sized kelp bulbs glint with the same sheen as seals. Timber deadheads in the bay, bobbing and breaching. Across the water, due south, the Olympic Peninsula is shrouded in sea mist, perfect cover for smugglers' coves.

Wind punches up, 40 kilometres per hour, forcing me to squint, my eyes tearing. I find a bench and watch the sea heave, churning in indigo. Trees grow in fortifications, reinforcing the shore. Below the brambles, beachside boulders form rough, rocky art. Light ratchets up, shifting gears in the sky, icy blue, the colour of lights all around. Water and sky have become their own distinct mood, frosty and aloof. I clamber down rock to the sea, the shore in stoney grooves. Glacial marks that resemble petrified logs, a Pleistocene boom, from when Rosie and her mates were splashing nearby.

I traipse around Victoria Harbour, west to Esquimalt. An hour of walking brings me to Saxe Point and Macaulay Point Parks. From the beach I climb through remnants of camas, bracken, cow parsnip, and broom, stuff that could make a fine wreath. I carry on where Brothers Islands stand in the bay, to the site of CFB Esquimalt's Old Gun Battery. There's a tunnel, low-ceilinged, carved through a hill, the look of the Hole in the Wall. I follow the tube to emerge at a crumbling brocade of concrete, the original battery, set here for the past hundred years.

Beyond the former artillery site, a mother strolls with her baby, and a man jogs with a dog on a leash. In the inlet, a cluster of boats, late-season fishing. An osprey wings by. Gulls scold. And a crow stands beside me and stares. Over thickets, a barn swallow swoops, orange with blue-black, nibbling things I can't see. Sun gently warms the cool air like a quilt being slowly drawn up.

I circle back around Victoria's downtown, following Dallas Road along the city's south shore. A Heermann's gull hovers past with a cry while a plover stands on a skerry, looking marooned. At a bend in the road, a sharp promontory points south.

I march to the end of the headland, where a sign indicates the Great Trail has begun, or concluded.

I head inland, bearing north, and tackle a hill, the feel of a game of ladders and snakes, only here I roll nothing but ladders. I climb to where a roughly trod path dead-ends partway up a massive rock bubble, a bald pate in the midst of the city. The stone underfoot is a mosaic of wrinkles, the elephant hide of old firs. I don't even plan my descent, simply climb. A scramble, a leap, a few stretching strides, and I summit, a small festive world at my feet. The wind here is surly and shoves me about, while carols still loop in my mind, echoes of seasonal harmonies.

The sea to the south is a cold flinty blue, now fanned into sundogs, a faint rainbow in mist. Beyond are Southern Gulf Islands and a hunk of the mainland. Cloud ribbons stream toward surf, what could be the launch of an ocean liner, passengers waving to loved ones. I imagine a vibrating horn, the excitement of travel. From here I believe I can see the whole city: the garlanded roof of Craigdarroch Castle, a hint of Centennial Square, the Legislative Building with its festive bright dome, the *Knowledge Totem* next to a massive sequoia. With a turn I see neighbourhood windows, icicle bulbs, reds and greens, silver blues, an array of flashing lights in some yards.

To descend from this peak, I have to keep moving forward. Crusty rock becomes steep narrow stairs, a pyramid-feel of altars and vertical worship. The smear of sunlight now almost looks sad, maybe worried the season is nearing an end, forgetting it'll return soon enough. Another solstice and calendar page. Gradually lengthening days and more light in the sky, rather than in windows and on trees.

At the moment, mind you, I could go for some cocoa and flannels, a holiday film and some candy. Recollecting every kind person and the shared festive feelings I've found through the season. Maybe listen for bells or a whistle through glass. Until then, I'll explore a bit more. Down the serpentine shore a breakwater beckons, a long finger crooking, *this way*. The structure is adorned in Salishan paintings, murals of the Songhees and Esquimalt. Called the Unity Wall, it's a welcome to travellers. The breakwater serves as moorage for cruise ships, although nothing's in port at the moment. From the street I follow the walkway, and stroll out to sea for a while. What strikes me here, elevated, effectively walking on water, is a change in the air. On the hill it was stuffy in fog. On the water it's icy but clear. No difference in wind, sun, or cloud. Simply air over water, another sea lung in crisp salination.

I return through Victoria Harbour, past the longhouse facade that gleamed a short while ago.

Lekwungen land, home to Songhees and Xwsepsum of the Coast Salish Nations. One more visit to the BC Museum, to the First Peoples Gallery and Totem Hall, the room featuring carvings from the Kwakwa̱ka̱'wakw, Heiltsuk, Nuxalk, Gitxsan, Haida, and Nuu-chah-nulth Nations. Once more I feel transported through the art, same as the paintings of Emily Carr, brushstroke forests, every colour of green, all this her muse, carvings and masks, history pre- and post-contact.

Now I'm at Jonathan Hunt Ceremonial House, the house of Chief Kwakwabalasami, Kwakwa̱ka̱'wakw Chief from Vancouver Island's northeast. This installation is the property of the Chief's family, although this exhibit is permanent, a complete ceremonial house, used by the Chief for potlatches in Alert Bay before being moved here to Victoria. The soft sound, aroma, and lighting leave me feeling I'm still on the water – another recollection, this time of year, on a ferry.

That particular trip we weren't slicing through fog, no imagined tornadoes or Dorothy. The sailing was the first of the day, my vehicle jammed between transport trucks, trailers, and rigs. With a takeaway coffee, I pulled on my toque and braved gale-force wind on the uppermost deck, where a rising sun gilded the strait. Something about the glint on the water, a wide wake of seafoam, had me feeling as though I was an Argonaut, a swamper on Jason's Hellenic crew, our quest for gold fleece, something festive we could snuggle in or use to wrap presents.

While I daydreamed, warming hands through my thin cup of coffee, the sea exploded directly off the port bow, more than a hundred seals thrashing the water, barking and diving. A feeding frenzy, perhaps, a bait-ball or shoal of herring. A spectacular show, better than Sea World or anything captured on film. One other passenger stayed there to see it, in the chill of that sunrise, watching nature displayed. With a smile and nod we shared in the moment, no parcels or wrapping, just connection and a gift unexpected. ❖

Sunset from Qualicum Bay

Clear Skies on Highway 19

ELK

Yeti Footprints, Parksville to Qualicum

Ahead of the Season at Telegraph Cove

Crossing the Salish Sea

Overleaf: Morning Rainbow, Esquimalt

Sea Star...for the Tree?

A SORT OF CONCLUSION

Celebration and Connection

Maybe it's that capture of the serendipitous, the gift of present moments that delineates seasons, beyond calendars or dates chosen to coincide with the turn of the planet. It's certainly much more than months: time linked to lions or lambs, showers and flowers, school commencing or ending in holidays. For in each delineation, borders blur, blend, and borrow, occasionally steal, melding memories while conjuring mysteries. That's what I see in these fragments, each season. Exploration and wonder, celebration and connection as well.

It's now the tail end of a traditional festive season and all that might mean – individually, collectively. The last of this current excursion as well. So I drive a bit more, then I walk, facing west, and now east, a glimpse of sunset, then home, wanting to absorb a bit more and to savour this amalgam of experiences. One more shoreline walk, one more ferry, passing smiles and nods. With things noticeably quieter, simmered down. Like a calm has descended.

Peacefulness. As though the season has finally accomplished its true objective.

Lingering cloud softens, retreats, leaving nothing but chill bands of sun, an echo of seasonal bells, a whisper of blue glass in a breeze. Someone developing wings, perhaps, or simply relearning to fly.

The solstice slips by, midwinter events, reminders of ancient traditions, as the day of celebration, for many, arrives. Then it passes. Music transitions once more. Carols trail off. And I hear "Fairytale of New York" for what's likely the last time this year, the vocal tumble that kicked off the season. Another calendar turn and perhaps resolutions, with the usual flood of new gym memberships. Days slowly lengthen. And a night sky of fireworks concludes with another round of "Auld Lang Syne," as though we've been cast in that radio play, real life in the midst of artistic depiction. Colour and sound. With a smile I raise a small glass, to nothing specific, a salute to most everything, and a toast to each one of us too. ❁

NAMES AND NARRATION

As I endeavour to do with each Season book, to the best of my ability I share names of regions and people in frequently used, anglicized, or phonetic translations of Indigenous language. Even though I've worked with experts, ongoing research reveals alternate spellings or definitions of words. While my own heritage is that of European settlers, having moved for opportunity or safety, my appreciation of the First Peoples to live on and live with this land fosters unending gratitude to each cultural keeper and guardian. And I remain privileged and thankful to consider this area part of my home.

Despite best efforts, each book I write, to a degree, imparts a settler perspective onto regional narrative. With this book in particular, and its delicate probe into faith and traditions, I hope that sincerity speaks to what we all feel, or aspire to, which is something I note with respect to writing of travel and memoir in general. Beyond spelling and pronunciation, words are subjective. We see the world through private and personal lenses. Yet it's my desire that these books might pose a few questions, even prompt revelation, along with a comfy escape, inspiration, and ideally a chuckle or two. In other words, a shared sliver of life.

In previous books I relayed an island vignette from another Pacific west coast, on Hawaii, where locals lay pieces of white coral on the dark lava ground, spelling out words of compassion: ALOHA, LOVE, HOPE. Every word pops, light against dark, while melding into the binding sentiments of kindness and compassion. Much like each place of worship I've been to and the people I've gotten to know, admire, and learn from, those common sentiments reign, irrespective of faith or belief. Another blur, shift of season, and, I like to believe, transition toward something better. Where commonality, blended narrative, and culture share common space, recognizing the fact that *all* space is shared. ❖

ACKNOWLEDGEMENTS

Writing memoir or travel is predominantly a personal endeavour, but creating a book takes a team. And for the hard-working team at Rocky Mountain Books, I'm most grateful: publisher Don Gorman, editors Joe Wilderson, Kirsten Craven, and Kelly Laycock, proofreader Peter Enman, art director Chyla Cardinal, sales representative Cory Manning, and the media efforts of Grace Gorman and James Faccinto. With extra thanks going to both Kirsten and Kelly for the time and care they put into making this book a pleasure to work on together.

The artwork you see is my own, photos I've taken and then digitally painted using a combination of customized applications. The map of Vancouver Island was created by Lara Minja of Lime Design, while together we added the commonly used place names I feel are most relevant to these particular excursions. Additional thanks go to Lara for making the entire book, like all our Season books, visually stunning.

People I've met, visited with, and learned from have clearly played an integral role in this journey. Thanks to Gayle, Angie, Ethan and Dawn, Khaled and Randa, Rabbi Bentzi and Blumie, Jennifer, Harj,

Yuka and Suzanne, Lena, Doug, Lauren and Martin, Jim, Stewart, Carol, Bridget, Sylvia, Crystal, Brian, Jesse, Lisa and Mallory, Polina, Kellie, Jeff and Jess, Karen, Peter, Linda, Jeannie, Laura, Frances, and even the clothing-optional sasquatch. With extra thanks to Reverend Stephen, to Mala, and to Nicola North and her art. Of course, my appreciation extends to the late Andy Williams and Shane MacGowan, no doubt harmonizing somewhere, maybe through mics of blue glass.

And as always my love goes to Deb, with thanks for so many remarkable seasons, and the festiveness all of them hold. ❁

ABOUT THE AUTHOR

Bill Arnott is the bestselling author of the Gone Viking travelogues, *A Perfect Day for a Walk*, its sequel, *A Perfect Day for a Walk by the Water*, and the award-winning Season memoirs: *A Season on Vancouver Island*, *A Season in the Okanagan*, and *A Festive Season on Vancouver Island*. He is a Travel Ambassador for *Canadian Geographic* and Adventure Canada, and for his expeditions received Fellowships at Britain's Royal Geographical Society and the Royal Canadian Geographical Society. When not trekking with a small pack and journal, armed with his laughably outdated camera phone, or showing off cooking skills as a culinary school dropout, Bill can be found on Canada's west coast, where he lives near the sea on Musqueam, Squamish, and Tsleil-Waututh land.

We would like to take this opportunity to acknowledge the Traditional Territories upon which we live and work. In Calgary, Alberta, we acknowledge the Niitsítapi (Blackfoot) and the people of the Treaty 7 region in Southern Alberta, which includes the Siksika, the Piikuni, the Kainai, the Tsuut'ina, and the Stoney Nakoda First Nations, including Chiniki, Bearpaw, and Wesley First Nations. The City of Calgary is also home to Métis Nation of Alberta, Region III. In Victoria, British Columbia, we acknowledge the Traditional Territories of the Lkwungen (Esquimalt and Songhees), Malahat, Pacheedaht, Scia'new, T'Sou-ke, and W̱SÁNEĆ (Pauquachin, Tsartlip, Tsawout, Tseycum) Peoples.